LEEDS TRANSPORT
ON POSTCARDS

by

Jim Soper

THE CAR TERMINUS KILLINGBECK.

The most prolific Leeds postcard publisher was William Bramley of Cross Gates who published from 8,000 to 9,000 postcards under the title of the Electric Light Printing Company. This is one of his finest transport cards and shows an 1899-built B.T-H. car at the tram terminus at the junction of York Road and Selby Road at Halton Dial. The tram is returning to Stanningley and the date is about 1906. In the background is the old toll house demolished in 1929 for road widening. *William Bramley*

Published by the Leeds Transport Historical Society 2012

A Society for the study and preservation of local passenger transport
Registered Charity No. 501642
Registered Address: 17 Church Street, Gildersome, Morley, Leeds, LS27 7AE

Printed by
The Amadeus Press, Cleckheaton, West Yorkshire, BD19 4TQ

Hardback ISBN 978-0-9510280-6-5
Soft cover ISBN 978-0-9510280-7-0

This is probably one of the best views of the many (over two dozen postcards) of the wooden arch that was erected at the City Square end of Wellington Street to mark the visit of King Edward VII and Queen Alexandra to Leeds in July 1908. The Phototype Company of Somerby Street published about 50 postcards of the event and included was this picture of the arch with Dick,Kerr car 278 bound for Pudsey, a handcart and a man mounting a bicycle. Workmen are putting the finishing touches to the arch.

Phototype Company P20

CONTENTS

THE LEEDS "PALS" BATTALION RECRUITING CAR (4).
Copyright

This card is from a series of eight cards published in 1914 of Dick,Kerr car 272 decorated as a "Leeds Pals" recruiting car.   The colour scheme was red, white and blue, with blue muslin covering much of the tram.   This is No. 4 of the series, the only one of a vertical format. See page 52 for card No.1 of the series.

Unknown publisher

INTRODUCTION

A number of booklets have appeared featuring Leeds on picture postcards, but this is the first attempt to give some details of an important commercial activity in Leeds, the publication and sale of picture postcards and in particular the way in which local transport in the city was depicted. Any conclusions drawn and opinions expressed are entirely the views and responsibility of the writer.

The picture postcard plays an important part in our understanding of the social history of Leeds and the country generally. Postcards were published nationally on every conceivable subject and local topography was very popular. Without postcards our knowledge of Edwardian Britain would be very much the poorer. Plain postcards with pre-printed half penny stamps were introduced in October 1870, but the picture postcard did not appear in Great Britain until 1 September 1894. On this day the Post Office allowed privately published cards to be sent by post. A one half penny stamp was attached to the back of the card with the address to which the card was to be sent; any message was written on the front of the card. Some cards had been sent before this date. Apart from official cards there had been some advertising cards and hand-drawn one-offs. In 1883 Germany was the first country to introduce postcards and the German "Gruss Aus" or "Greetings From" cards were very popular. Some of the early British cards were of this type. At first there were Court cards of a smaller size (3½ x 4½ in.) than the later larger post card. These were monochrome or coloured with a single view or multiview with a space for a message. The earliest known British picture postcard was posted in Scarborough on 15 September 1894, a fortnight after the new Post Office ruling. It was published by E.T.W. Dennis of Scarborough. The earliest Leeds card so far found bears a postmark of 25 January 1897. By June 1898 normal size postcards (3½ x 5½ in.) appeared in Leeds. This was some 17 months before the GPO "official" date of November 1899.

Local transport appeared on Leeds postcards from 1898. German-printed "Greetings From" cards show trams in the Leeds city centre – albeit German single deck electric cars. Trams dominated the streets of Leeds in the period before the First World War and after, and naturally most of the transport cards show trams, horse-drawn traffic and occasionally early motor cars. A small number of specially posed photographs were taken of the first Leeds motor buses and trackless cars and they appeared as picture postcards. These have been previously published by the LTHS and hence there are few bus and trackless postcards in this work. Some enterprising local photographers set up their tripods at a tram terminus and photographed every tram and crew that came along. These postcards were rarely on general sale and probably no more than half a dozen copies of each were produced. Many commercial firms produced postcards of vehicles for advertising purposes. Shopkeepers had their shops and vehicles photographed as advertisements. Many of the railway stations in the Leeds area are seen on postcards, but railway locomotives, although a large number of cards were produced, are rarely local to Leeds. Transport continued to appear on postcards until the traditional postcard's demise in the 1960's.

The information in this work is based on the study of over 8,000 Leeds postcards in various collections and several thousands of cards of the villages around Leeds. Details of known publishers are included in the Appendix with estimates of the numbers and types of postcard they produced. Unfortunately about 25% to 30% of cards seen have no indication of the publisher, including some relatively large series – over 50-100 cards – in some cases. Details of publishers have been obtained mainly from local directories and census returns.

Serial numbers by some publishers suggest that they produced large numbers of cards. However, these may have been in very small quantities for some cards, and they will not have survived the passage of time. A large number of the early photographic cards are now badly faded or damaged, in particular those by Baker, Bramley, Century Photographic Company, Colonial Series, H. Graham Glen, Parkinson & Roy, Phototype Company, Taylors etc. Later photographic cards and reprints tended to be sepia toned and not prone to fading. Many faded cards have been computer enhanced to restore them to their original condition.

From 1 January 1902 the Post Office allowed divided backs on postcards providing space for both the address of the recipient and a written message. Hence the conventional picture post card was born. Early cards were monochrome or coloured and it was not until about 1903 with the introduction of real photographic or "RP" cards that an Edwardian postcard collecting craze begun. Most families had their treasured postcard albums and the womenfolk appear to have sent most of the cards and been the principal collectors.

How many Leeds picture postcards were published? Prior to 1902 there were probably no more than about 200 to 300 cards with undivided backs. No one knows and probably will never know the number of Leeds cards published after 1902, but it was certainly in excess of 15,000 and probably over 20,000. Some information has been obtained from "Picture Post Card Monthly" magazine and the Valentine Archive. The Leeds Transport Historical Society would like to thank I.Ballantine, A.Cowell, I.M.Dougill, L.Fish, J.Guest, J.M.Hindes, J.G.Kaye, D.Rayner, R.Soper and the writer's sons-in-law, D.Spencer and J.Wales in helping with this work. Justin Wales has carried out extensive research into the census returns and St. Catherine's House records. As far as is known most of the illustrations have not appeared in other books, but a number of previously published views which form an important part of the story are included. We have inspected thousands of photographs, but have had difficulty in identifying the early motor cars. There were over 5,000 different makes, many copies of each other.

The LTHS is aware that there are many postcard collectors that we have not been able to contact. If any readers can point out any inaccuracies and can provide further information to add to these notes and appendices we would be very grateful to hear from them. Any information received will be included in a possible future second volume and fully acknowledged.

J.Soper, Leeds Transport Historical Society,   August 2012

Some of the first postcards of Leeds were German-printed "Gruss Aus" or "Greetings From" cards. This one is postmarked 23 June 1898 and was sent by a German tourist to his homeland. Eveleigh Bishop of Leeds was the publisher and he published at least two other similar postcards, (Nos.2736 and 2805), but they do not have any transport interest. These Leeds "Greetings From" cards were published in fairly large numbers and were still being sold in 1908. *Eveleigh Bishop, Leeds, No. 2806*

An enlargement from the card above showing details of the "local" Leeds transport. It shows some "artist's licence" with right hand running German single deck electric trams with bow collectors.

THE LEEDS POSTCARD BUSINESS

The Leeds postcard business was extremely competitive and at times cut throat. The publishers were many in number, some published thousands of cards and others a few only. The business started quietly enough with imported cards from overseas and initially the postcards were used mainly by foreign tourists. Eveleigh Bishop of Briggate and James Glen of Batley, a photographer, appear to have been the first of the local publishers. They were soon followed by Henry Graham Glen of Wortley (James' younger brother) who by August 1898 was publishing monochrome single and multiview Court cards, mostly printed in Germany, of popular locations in Leeds.

German printers dominated the first few years of the postcard business. There were price wars and in the period before 1914 Germany offered severe competition to all British postcard publishers. Leeds was an important printing centre and competition with Germany came in 1903-4 with the emergence of several Leeds postcard publishers. W. & T. Gaines of Bankfield Terrace, Burley, Parkinson & Roy of Kelsall Street, the Phototype Company of Somerby Street, (off Ventnor Street), and J.S. Savile & Co. of Headingley were the most notable. National publishers, E.T.W. Dennis of Scarborough, (by 1899) J. Valentine of Dundee (by 1901), Rotary Photographic Company and William Ritchie & Sons of Edinburgh with its 'Reliable' Series (1903) appeared and stationers, W.H. Smith & Sons and Chemists, Boots, began publishing Leeds postcards about 1904-5.

The inauguration of City Square in Leeds on 16 September 1903 seems to be the catalyst that induced twin brothers Walter and Tom Gaines to start publishing postcards. They must have sold a large number of the event. Their first cards were all of the monochrome or coloured type. H. Graham Glen was one of the first Leeds publishers to produce real photographic or "RP" cards, as early as 1903. Bamforth of Holmfirth also published a few Leeds RP cards in 1903 and in 1905 the Phototype Company issued about 200-300 RP views of Leeds and suburbs. A. & G. Taylor of London, Leeds and Bradford, also published RP Leeds views in the 1904-6 period. All of the early Leeds postcards were of popular locations, i.e. principal buildings, main city centre streets, Roundhay Park, Kirkstall Abbey etc. Suburban postcards were not generally introduced until about 1903-4 and it was around 1903 that some of the post offices began to publish postcards of their immediate area. J.N. Richardson of Headingley Post Office was probably the first and was publishing monochrome cards as early as July 1903. Many of the post offices and stationers in Leeds published postcards of their local area from one or two cards to more than 100 in some cases.

It soon became very competitive in the Leeds postcard world. During 1905 the Phototype Company had been quietly taking large numbers of photographs in Leeds and its suburbs and also in many surrounding villages. In April and May 1906 it flooded the market with the simultaneous publication of a thousand new RP Leeds cards plus some in outer areas. The other major Leeds publishers, Gaines, Glen, Parkinson & Roy, Savile and Taylor were effectively put out of the RP business. H. Graham Glen had already published about 3,000 to 4,000 views, some of Leeds, but mainly of other areas of Yorkshire and Lancashire and as far afield as Belfast, Blackpool, Carlisle, Middlesbrough. Morecambe, Preston and Scunthorpe etc. Glen cards of outside areas appear to have been published in very small numbers, probably no more than half a dozen for each. Glen, Bramley, Gaines and Chadwick (see later) seem to have been the only Leeds publishers to publish cards of districts outside of the Yorkshire area. After 1906 most of Glen's activities were concentrated on the publication of coloured versions of his existing RP views. Similarly Gaines published few new postcards after 1906. The firm published over 80 RP cards of Leeds and district, but did not attempt to compete with Phototype and later Gaines postcards were mainly confined to coloured views and postcards of special events. Savile had published about 450 mainly monochrome postcards, some of Leeds, but mostly of distant villages, many in the East Riding of Yorkshire. No new Savile cards appeared after 1906.

The national publishers also joined the Leeds RP scene. At first they had published monochrome and coloured cards only, but with the publication of RP type cards in vast numbers, forced all the big Leeds publishers out of business. Beginning with J.Valentine of Dundee by 1905, the Rotary Photo Company of London the following year and Reliable in 1908 they produced high quality photographic type cards of popular locations in Leeds. These were created by a printing process and unlike normal RP cards they were on a better quality paper and did not fade. Boots, the chemists, and W.H. Smith & Son, newsagents and stationers, also published large numbers of RP cards at this time. Initially the Phototype Company must have received large orders, but the subject matter was mainly confined to obscure suburban streets and small Yorkshire villages for which there would be limited sales. It would appear that repeat orders were not forthcoming and the firm went out of business abruptly in the middle of 1909. Research has not yet discovered the reason. The premises in Somerby Street were vacated, but new postcards continued to be published for two or three years, probably by the photographer working from home. No indication of a publisher has been found on these later cards.

Gaines and Glen had concentrated on the production of coloured cards, but topographical cards of this type became less popular in the late Edwardian period. In an attempt to boost sales, highly decorative coloured cards some laminated, in the form of ovals or circles with decorative borders were introduced by Reliable, Gaines, Glen, Taylors and others. Gaines and one or two other firms added gold glitter to some cards. Card decoration increased and in 1912 two Leeds firms, Fowler and Nicholson produced some cards with rather garish coloured borders and Machan of Wakefield published some gold colour cards. Machan's, Fowler's and Nicholson's elaborate decorative cards were printed in Germany and must have been expensive to produce. They were short lived. Earlier, monochrome cards had also gone out of favour, collectors preferring the coloured card, but they now turned to the photographic card. Both Glen and Gaines ceased to publish new cards en masse about 1909 and 1911 respectively. Glen, however, remained in business as a photographer until about 1933 and continued to publish a small number of new cards until about 1928. Gaines published one or two new cards until 1914. Following the demise of Phototype and seeing a potential business opportunity, a Leeds photographer, Ernest R. Slater of Basinghall Street began, about August 1909, a "fine art printing and publishing" business. He published over 150 cards and also a number of decorative coloured cards of a similar type to those of Reliable and others.

The Phototype Company in 1909, Parkinson & Roy in 1910 and Savile in 1906, had ceased to trade and there was a gap in the large scale production of postcards of Yorkshire villages. This was filled by an enterprising photographer, William Bramley of Cross Gates, who published postcards under the title of the Electric Light Printing Company. As early as 1905 he had published a few coloured and RP cards of Cross Gates, Garforth, Seacroft, Whitkirk and a few other villages near to Leeds. He had also produced some RP postcards of various Leeds carnivals etc. He was very industrious and expanded his activities with many RP postcards of Yorkshire villages and small towns. Whereas the Phototype Company had photographed about 150 Yorkshire villages and towns, Savile just over 40 and Parkinson & Roy about the same number, Bramley covered 300-400, including many of the villages and towns in Yorkshire to the north and east of Leeds. He was the most prolific of the Leeds publishers. He did not attempt to compete with the national publishers and avoided Leeds city centre, but did produce a few cards of some of the north east suburbs. Retailers Boots had ceased to publish Leeds cards by 1914, but Valentine continued throughout the First World War and similarly Reliable was publishing Leeds cards until the late 'twenties. A new national publisher appeared by August 1920. This was Lilywhite Ltd., of Halifax, a firm which published Leeds postcards until the early 1960's.

The postcard collecting hobby reached its zenith about 1907 and then slowly declined. In October 1915 the War Office issued a warning to publishers and traders not to sell postcards showing maps, prominent buildings and monuments "which may be useful to enemy aircraft." There is no evidence that the Leeds traders heeded this instruction. A severe blow came in June 1918 when the postage rate was increased from ½d. to 1d. Another blow in July 1921 when the postal rate was further raised to 1½d. effectively "killed off" the postcard trade in Leeds. The 'Yorkshire Post' said that sales had plummeted by 50 to 80%.
"This applies most particularly to pictorial view cards which are bought almost exclusively for the purpose of posting, and not so much to photographs of celebrities which are usually bought for collections. The public will simply not pay 1 ½ d. postage."
'Yorkshire Post', 21 July 1921.

The 1½d. charge was short lived and reverted to 1d. less than a year later. A modest revival in postcard purchasing occurred. This was in spite of a countrywide depression at the time and the introduction of the Kodak Brownie box camera which enabled people to take their own views. In 1922 and 1923 two new Leeds publishers appeared. The first was Harry Burniston of Francis Street, Chapeltown, who published over 650 high quality photographic type cards. He was followed by Arthur Steven of Chapel Allerton Post Office. Steven was not new to postcard production. He was a keen photographer and from about 1905 had published about a thousand RP postcards under the title of the "Steven Series" - views of North Yorkshire villages centred on Thirsk. His Thirsk enterprise was called "Stevens & Co. Thirsk." It seems that the severe recession and collapse of the postcard trade in the early 'twenties forced Steven to take up a more secure business. He became the most active of the small Leeds publishers. Working from home (latterly 7 Wensley View, Chapel Allerton) he produced about 150-200 RP cards within a half mile radius of his post office. He continued to publish the Thirsk area cards and was still publishing "Steven Series" cards until his death in 1956. They were printed in his distinctive "left hand" style and on the same paper as his Chapel Allerton cards.

The late 'twenties and early thirties was a fairly quiet period so far as Leeds postcards were concerned, but a Bradford publisher, Matthews, appeared and published about 10,000 good quality cards including some of Leeds. The collecting hobby, however, became less popular and by 1930 most of the local small Leeds post offices, except Steven and one or two others, had ceased to issue cards. Burniston did not publish any new cards after 1934, but cards by national publishers Valentine and Lilywhite were available throughout the 'thirties. A new national publisher called Excel appeared about 1928 and published about 80 RP type postcards of popular locations in Leeds. Bamforth also published some new Leeds cards in the 'thirties. An old established Leeds firm of photographers, Charles Pickard & Sons of Park Lane did the same and in 1938 Richards of Strensall, near York, published a large number of Yorkshire postcards including over 400 RP cards of Leeds. These included many suburban views. Coloured, sepia and monochrome postcards of Leeds had been published in large numbers until about 1912. For the following forty years, however, very few of these cards were produced. The photographic card reigned supreme.

After the Second World War, two new publishers appeared, Chadwick of Roundhay Road in 1948 and a national publisher, J.F.Lawrence, of an unknown address in 1955. Both published printed photographic type cards. National publishers Bamforth, Excel, Frith of Reigate, Judges of Hastings, Photochrom Company of Tunbridge Wells, Salmon of Sevenoaks, Walter Scott Ltd. of Bradford, Raphael Tuck & Sons of London and Valentine published some Leeds cards in the 1950's. Their photographic postcards were on sale until the early 1960's. Steven was one of the last of the local publishers, but Chadwick was the last in the late 1960's.

Colour photography was in its infancy in the 1940's and the only colour transparency film available in the U.K. was Dufaycolor, a dense film not very suitable for colour reproduction. In 1953 new films, Kodachrome (U.S.A), Ferraniacolor (Italy) and Agfacolor (Germany) were introduced. These revolutionised postcard production and revived the coloured postcard. They signalled the birth of the "modern" topographical postcard. In 1952 Dennis had published a few rather poor hand coloured views of Leeds, but colour printing improved and ten years later the firm produced about 150 good quality coloured postcards of Leeds in three versions and was still publishing new Leeds cards in the 1990's. Many were multiviews. Bamforth, Chadwick, Frith, Judges, Salmon, Scott and Tuck also published coloured postcards of Leeds in the 'sixties and 'seventies. Most were of the larger Continental (4⅛ in. x 5⅞ in.) than the standard postcard size. In 1950 The Photochrom Company and Tuck had published a few sepia views of Leeds, but monochrome cards did not reappear. Valentine published its last RP card in 1955 and apart from a small number of "Collocolour" cards published in its "L" and "M" series did not enter the colour postcard business. The Valentine Archive shows that after July 1966 the firm ceased to publish any new postcards. The photographic card did not "die" easily. About 1960-1 Lilywhite Ltd. published 25 large format photographic cards with deckled edges. Bamforth, Chadwick and Lawrence produced a few cards of the same type. These were the last RP postcards to be published of Leeds

Early Postcards

31/12/01

Headingley

many thanks for the redirected letters. Am having a nice time. I hope you are better.

Briggate, Leeds.

A Happy New Year.   Pollie

Postcards of steam trams are rare, but this one is especially interesting as Pollie posted the card on 31 December 1901. From 1 January 1902 cards with divided backs were permitted and both the message and address could be on the back of the card. The tram engine was built by Thomas Green & Son Ltd. of North Street, Leeds, and the trailer by Milnes & Co. of Birkenhead.   *H. Graham Glen, Wortley*

BOAR LANE (WEST BAR), LEEDS.

4/3/03

Dear Sissy. Do not think I have forgotten you
Nellie   ARTHUR HICKS, LEEDS.

Nellie was behind the times when she sent this rather poignant message to Sissy in 1903. She was still writing on the front of the postcard. The trams are a B.T-H car of the 133-182 series and steam tram trailer No.63. The card was published about 1901 for Arthur Hicks of Leeds, by E.T.W. Dennis of Scarborough in its "Dainty Series". At least 24 printed cards with blue skies were produced. *E.T.W.Dennis*

The Post Office, Leeds.

RELIABLE [WH] SERIES.

A Reliable postcard, (published 1903, photographed 1901) of the Leeds General Post Office.   On the left is a cab awaiting passengers.   On the right Milnes horse tram No.50 and another car at the City Square terminus of the Burley Road horse tram route.   The Burley Road horse trams were replaced by electric cars on 3 August 1901.   There were 14 horse trams of this type, all purchased in 1897-1898 and withdrawn in late 1901.   One, No.107, is currently being restored by the LTHS.   *Reliable Series*

Made by W. H., Berlin. No. 3105.

Briggate from Duncan Street, Leeds.

When held against the light the windows on this "Hold to Light" postcard glow.   This is one of a series of six cards published of Leeds by W. Hagelberg of Berlin in 1903. Hagelberg published "Hold to Light" cards world wide and this one is based on a H.Graham Glen view dating from 1901.   The card shows an 1899-built B.T-H car 162, a Thomas Green steam tram engine and Milnes trailer.   This neatly written card was sent from Bertie to Master Joey Myers of Crawford College, Maidenhead.   Bertie said he was in form IVA and his teacher was Mr. Warren.   The card is postmarked 4 October 1903.
W.Hagelberg, Berlin. Series 3105

Private Horse-drawn Transport

The more opulent residents of Leeds had their own private carriages complete with coachman in the traditional top hat. When the horse-drawn carriage gave way to the motor car, the coachman was often employed as a chauffeur. This 1905 view was taken in Headingley Lane. *Phototype Company 311*

Postcards of donkey carts are not common. This one was used by "Old Reynolds" of Bramham, a village character in the late nineteenth century. Robert Reynolds (1827-1914) lived in Back Street, Bramham. The card, postmarked 25 December 1904, was sent by Harry Harland, a harness maker of Bramham, who wrote that he had made the special harness. Parkinson & Roy was one of the first firms to publish postcards of this village about 12 miles from Leeds. *Parkinson & Roy Studios, Leeds*

Competition from national publishers and the production of over a thousand postcards of minor streets in Leeds and many postcards of small Yorkshire villages were probably the main cause of the demise of the Phototype Company in 1909. After big initial sales there were possibly few repeat orders. Many of the street scenes were unanimated, but in this view of Hill Top Mount in Harehills, the photographer has tried to make the postcard more "saleable" by placing a horse and cart at an angle across the road. Although of interest to social historians, one could speculate as to how many copies of this 1905 postcard would have been sold; 20 to 30 perhaps, but unlikely to be more than 50.   *Phototype Company 761*

This view is near to that above, and was one of several taken, by the Phototype photographer for Harrison & Tate, stationers of Harehills Parade. To make the postcard more interesting a small gig has been placed at an angle across Harehills Avenue. Card 762 of nearby Shepherds Lane also includes a horse and gig, but card 759 of Ellers Road does not have any posed vehicles.   *Phototype Company 764*

Commercial horse-drawn transport

Joshua Tetley & Son, the well known Leeds brewers, were normally associated with heavy drays, but this small cart (No.120 in the Tetley's "fleet") was shown, with a beautifully caparisoned white horse, at some unknown event. The card is postmarked 24 July 1910 and was sent to Miss Francis Akroyd in Morecambe, but does not carry a message.   *Unknown publisher*

This traditional brewery dray was used by The Armley Brewery Ltd., brewers and maltsters of Armley Road. The firm existed from about 1898 to 1928.   *Unknown publisher*

This spotless Leeds Industrial Co-operative Society Laundry Department van was exhibited at Morley Carnival on 20 June 1914. The laundries were in Osmondthorpe Lane and Gelderd Road. The man in white coat is believed to have been named T.Lawn. *Unknown publisher*

From this humble beginning the giant supermarket chain ASDA was born. In 1892 John Ledger Hindell started business as a milkman at 51 New Park Street, Park Lane, Leeds. Beginning in 1909 he gradually expanded his business and in 1920 it was known as Hindell's Dairies. Shortly afterwards a group of local farmers took over and it became Hindell's Dairy Farmers Ltd., processing milk and meat to an increasing number of customers. In 1949 the firm was floated as "Associated Dairies and Farm Stores Ltd." The photograph of Hindell's milk cart is believed to be taken in the area of Park Lane about 1910. *D.Beck*

This is an advertising postcard used by the Cambrian Vinegar Co. of Elland Road, Leeds. On 27 August 1905, the firm's agent, William Birbeck, wrote that he would call upon Mr.R. Lord Gifford of Blackburn on Thursday next 30th inst. The dray is being loaded with barrels of vinegar. The firm existed from about 1880 to 1960 when the premises were demolished.   *Cambrian Vinegar Company*

This cart with straw covered floor was owned by James Webster who was delivering produce to his shop at 253 Dewsbury Road, Leeds, There is poultry and many rabbits for sale.   The chalk-written notice reads: "Owing to the open weather, rabbits are very cheap".   The Webster family occupied this shop from about 1902 to the outbreak of the Second World War.   *Unknown publisher, Courtesy L.Fish*

11

This superbly painted cart was owned by dairyman, Alfred Bateman of Holbeck. He was at 25 Recreation Grove and later 35 Brown Lane, Holbeck, from about 1902 to 1930. This photograph was probably taken about 1905.
Unknown publisher, Courtesy L.Fish

The Bramley Steam Laundry existed from about 1901 to 1912. John William Lodge was the manager and at first the laundry was at Eightlands Lane, Town Street, Bramley, and from about 1905 at Aston Mount, Bramley.   This advertising postcard shows two of the firm's carts.
Bramley Steam Laundry

Wagonettes and Omnibuses

This wagonette outing was made by members of the Bethel Congregational Church, Wortley, Leeds, about 1905. The Reverend Booth is standing near the horses' heads. The ladies on the wagonette have similar features and were probably sisters – quads? The wagonette was owned by the Leeds firm of Chapman's, cab, omnibus and wagonette proprietors, established in 1885.   *Unknown publisher*

On the back of this fine postcard is written, "Our day trip out from Chapeltown, Leeds, May 17 1908." The writer has been unable to find exactly where the photograph was taken,   but it is believed to be in the Sheepscar area. There is no identification on the wagonette.   *Unknown publisher*

This postcard was sent from Stanningley on 20 September 1906 to Messrs. Clark, Hall Atkinson, clothiers, Park Lane, Leeds, with a message from Mr. Hudson of Stanningley, "Will call tomorrow night with macintosh." It is surprising that a postcard sent to a commercial firm has survived the passage of time. It shows Hollings' wagonette at an unknown location. There are also advertisement boards for the Yorkshire Post and Yorkshire Evening Post. *Unknown publisher*

George Horsfall, omnibus and wagonette proprietor of Disraeli Place, Dewsbury Road, ran wagonettes for private hire until the coming of the motor charabanc in the early 1920's. This 1905 view was taken at the King's Arms, 117 Dewsbury Road. The pub was at the junction with Addington Street. The driver is Willie Harrison and at the horses' heads is Walter Horsfall. *Parkinson & Roy Studios, Leeds*

Although these two wagonettes are drawn up at The Arabian Horse at Aberford on the Great North Road, it was never a coaching inn in the stage coach days. The Royal Mail coach changed horses at the Swan Hotel, Aberford, but other coaches changed at Ferrybridge and Wetherby. At 17 miles this was the longest stage on the Great North Road. Postmarked 21 July 1910, the postcard was sent from Jeannie to her sister Mrs. Gregory at Bishop Auckland. It was the start of a return journey to Dewsbury from a picnic on "Tuesday last week" (12 July) .   *Unknown publisher*

The Hunslet Carr horse bus service was inaugurated on 17 April 1865 and stables for the horses were built at the then new Bay Horse Hotel in Woodhouse Hill Road. This was the last local horse bus service in Leeds and the photograph was taken on 1 June 1905 the final day of operation. There were two bus proprietors working the service, James Gill and Thomas Bean, and this is Gill's bus. At least two other postcards were published of this event.   *Unknown publisher*

Probably the event which generated the most postcards in Leeds was the visit of H.M. King Edward VII and his Queen to open Leeds University on 7 July 1908.   Over 200 postcards were published by various firms. The processional route from Harewood House to the University was elaborately decorated and there were three triumphal arches and several "lesser" arches.   This arch was at the city boundary at Moortown and shows a horse and gig posed broadside across Harrogate Road.   *Unknown publisher*

This triumphal arch was erected at the end of Methley Drive, Chapel Allerton. Behind the tram pole is the roof of the then brand new Chapeltown tram depot.   *Phototype Company P8*

The Phototype Company of Somerby Street published over 50 postcards of the Royal Visit including this view of a small arch at the bottom of Woodhouse Lane. Portland Crescent is on the left and the tram in the distance is Greenwood & Batley car No.23 bound for Hyde Park.   *Phototype Company P23*

The Royal carriage leaving Leeds University after the opening ceremony. *W. & T. Gaines*

Leeds Mercury.   Childrens Pageant, Roundhay Park, LEEDS TERCENTENARY CELEBRATIONS   No 510

Harry Burniston, one of the major Leeds postcard publishers in the 1920's, published 22 postcards (Nos.506-527) of the Leeds Tercentenary Celebrations in 1926. Most were from 'Leeds Mercury' or 'Yorkshire Evening Post' photographs and were mainly of the Children's Pageant in Roundhay Park. Included was this view showing an imitation sedan chair "In the days of Queen Anne".
H. Burniston No. 510

"Quakers", BRAMLEY CARNIVAL, May 4th 1912 (9).

The annual May Bramley Carnival was one of the most popular Leeds carnivals in the decade before the First World War and generated over 100 postcards by different publishers.   For the Carnival of 4 May 1912 the Quakers had a car. Although in the Phototype Company style, there is no indication of a publisher on this postcard.
Unknown publisher

This postcard, probably of the 1907 Carnival, shows part of a procession in Bramley Town Street. Three of Ben Dixon's removal carts are carrying passengers and in the background is tramcar 85, a "reguiar" on the Bramley and Rodley tram route in this period. *Unknown publisher*

The villages of Cross Gates, Halton and Seacroft combined efforts with their May Carnivals. This undated postcard shows the May Queen's cart and is believed to be in Seacroft village. *JIV?*

Weddings and Funerals

A sailors' wedding about 1912.   A group of sailors are "towing" this landaulette, U 1854, with the bride and groom seated in the back.   The vehicle appears to be a Siddeley.   The location may be in the Belle Vue Road area. *Unknown publisher*

The Queen's Motor Company of Burley advertising wedding landaulettes for hire.   The distinctive shouldered radiators indicate that both U 1266 and U 2320 were manufactured by the Standard Motor Co. of Coventry.   Believed to be models 11 and 12, they had powerful 50 horse power six-cylinder engines. The date is about 1913.

Unknown publisher

TEL. 21168. **J. A. & L. BARKER.** 4. GREENMOUNT ST.. BEESTON HILL. **LEEDS.** TEL. 21168.

ONE OF OUR FLEET OF SUPER SALOON CARS.
AVAILABLE FOR WEDDINGS. Etc.

In the 1930's J.A. & L.Barker of Beeston Hill used this Sleeve valve Daimler for weddings. The car is photographed outside Adel Church.

Lilywhite Ltd. for J.A. & L.Barker

In the period from about 1900 to 1908 James Hillyard of 42 Ellerby Lane, a member of the "Leeds United Undertaker's Association", used a black horse and this nicely painted cart to carry his coffins.
Unknown publisher

Harry Thackray of Beeston was in business as a joiner and undertaker from about 1905 to 1921. This postcard shows Harry with hearse outside his premises at 37 Town Street, Beeston. The date is about 1914 and it is believed that this was the first motor hearse in Leeds. *Unknown publisher*

Richard Langford of Bramley was a popular Leeds tram driver who on 14 March 1911 was run over and killed by a tram at Bramley Town End. Shortly before, he had been to the railway station to say goodbye to a brother who was leaving for Canada. His work colleagues ensured he had a big send off and a few black bordered postcards were published of the event. *C.C. Vevers, Bramley*

There were many cycle makers in Leeds and Thomas Rigby of Hyde Park made a cycle called "The Wrangthorn", named after the nearby Wrangthorn Church. He was in business from about 1900 to 1911. The building on the photograph still exists.   See also page 117.   *Unknown publisher*

Walker's butcher's shop was a few doors away from Rigby's above, and it seems likely that his delivery bicycles would have been made by Rigby.   *Unknown publisher. Courtesy L.Fish*

Albert Irving Greenwood was one of the major early cycle, motor cycle and motor car dealers in Leeds. In 1896 he opened a business at 17 Woodhouse Lane and became an agent for many brands. He soon expanded and opened premises at 39-41 Guildford Street. This fine advertising card of the Guildford Street premises has been loaned by L. Fish. Greenwood's name was picked out in gilt. The firm was still in business in 1915, but ceased to trade soon afterwards. *A. I. Greenwood. Courtesy L.Fish*

This is the first meet of the Cross Gates and District Motor Cycling Club on 30 March 1912. The motor cycles are lined up outside the Brown Cow Inn at Whitkirk. Early motor cycles are difficult to identify viewed end on, but the two on the left are a then new Matchless V twin and a 1911 Singer. Like the firm's sewing machines, Singer motor cycles were well constructed. *W. Bramley, Cross Gates*

At first motor cycles were in effect motorised bicycles and were often unreliable. U 343 was an example and it appears to be a "Flying Monarch", the first motor cycle made by cycle maker Frank Morrish & Co. of Bristol. The many loose cables and tubes indicate that it could have been unsafe to ride.
Unknown publisher, Courtesy I. Ballantine

For the Leeds Tercentenary of 1926, the then new firm, Watson Cairns, motor cycle and cycle dealers of Lower Briggate, published two postcards of this float made up of a motor cycle and side car.   It shows UM 1600, a Royal Enfield of a new 346cc OHV single design by Ted Pardoe. The model was exhibited at Olympia in November 1925. On the float was a new Rudge Whitworth 500cc four valve motor cycle. Watson Cairns ceased to trade in 1997.   *Watson Cairns Ltd.*

"Dad" and his two children on what appears to be a brand new BSA about 1928.
Unknown Publisher, Courtesy I Ballantine.

In the 1920's the Brownie Box Camera was popular and many pictures were taken of the family motor cycle and side car. UM 8231 was a 350 cc A.J.S. and owned by the writer's father, William Henry Soper, who is pictured on this view taken at Arthington on 5 September 1929. In those leisurely days the only protection required was a heavy waterproof coat - no helmet, goggles, gloves or boots. *Author*

This car, U 311, must be the most photographed motor car in Edwardian Leeds. It was a French 1902-3 Panhard Levassor rear entrance tonneau. Panhard won many races and their cars were very popular at the time. The car was owned by Joseph Sydney Savile of Headingley and was used by both him and Walter and Tom Gaines to take photographers to villages in various parts of Yorkshire. It turns up on several postcards. Presumably Savile is the driver on this card. He seems pleased with the car and it appears to be the occasion when it was "launched".

J.S. Savile & Co. 336

U 311 adds interest to what is a rather boring 1905 view of Harrogate Road, Harewood.
J.S.Savile & Co. 410

No. 20   TONG LANE, TONG.   W. & T. GAINES, LEEDS

Gaines' took great pains in composing this photograph of Tong, near Bradford. What was an ordinary road has been transformed into an interesting photograph. U 311 has been positioned at an angle and the people have also been carefully placed. The postcard was published in 1909-10, but the photograph was almost certainly taken in 1905. *W. & T. Gaines Photographic Series No.20*

GARTON-ON-THE-WOLDS.   291.

The Panhard Levassor U 311 must have been one of the first motor cars to be seen in this small Yorkshire Wolds village and the locals have come out to have a look. *J.S. Savile & Co. 291*

Parkinson & Roy used this chauffeur-driven car, A 4062, a London-registered brand new six cylinder "noiseless" Napier Tonnea. The Napier was the most admired British car before Rolls Royce took over the top spot. It was the first car to adopt a successful production six cylinder engine and the first British car to reach 100 mph and a World Record Holder. A 4062 was used to take photographs of Garforth in 1904. Like nearly all Parkinson & Roy RP postcards, this was badly faded and has been digitally restored to its original condition. The card carries a postmark of 13 September 1904. *Parkinson & Roy, Leeds*

The garage and car hire premises of the Kirkstall Motor Company were at 58 Commercial Road, Kirkstall, and the firm existed from about 1908 to 1916. This line up shows M 14, U 1045, U 1199, and U 763. We think U 1045 is a Scout manufactured by the Scout Motor Company of Salisbury, but have not been able to identify the other cars. *Unknown publisher*

THE PERPLEXITY OF POLICEMAN P99.—Agitated and perspiring member of the force (who has been instructed to take the numbers of all passing motor-cars): "Er—A102?—P201?—LB976—7002—A. B. C. D.—12——— Where am I now? This means dismissal!"   [*Reproduced by permission from "THE MOTOR."*]

POLICE TRAPS ARE USELESS WITHOUT "TARMITE."

It is not clear from this advertising postcard what "Tarmite" was supposed to do. It was manufactured by The Yorkshire & Lincolnshire Tar Distillation Co. of Standard Buildings, Leeds. We think it was a binding agent for the macadam road surface to prevent dust which is blinding the police constable. The firm also made creosote. The card is postmarked 5 August 1908.
Yorkshire & Lincolnshire Tar Distillation Co.

COOKRIDGE SERVICE STATION, COOKRIDGE, NEAR LEEDS.

A 1930's postcard of Cookridge Garage. *Unknown publisher*

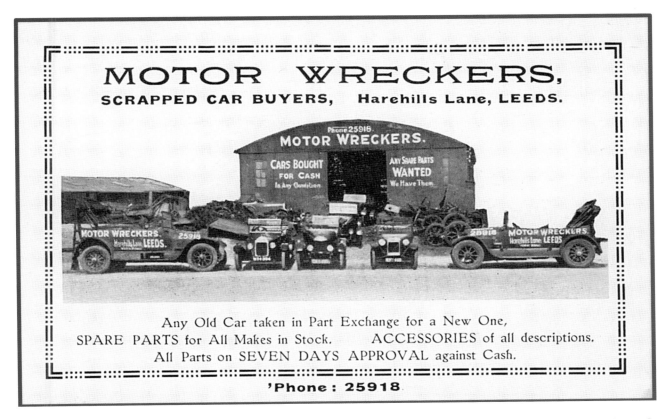

This is an advertising card published by Motor Wreckers of Harehills Lane about 1930. The sole proprietor was A. Goodhind. Soon after, the firm moved to 400a York Road, Leeds. The car in the middle of the photograph is a "bull nose" Morris Cowley or Oxford and on the left an Austin Heavy 12.
Motor Wreckers

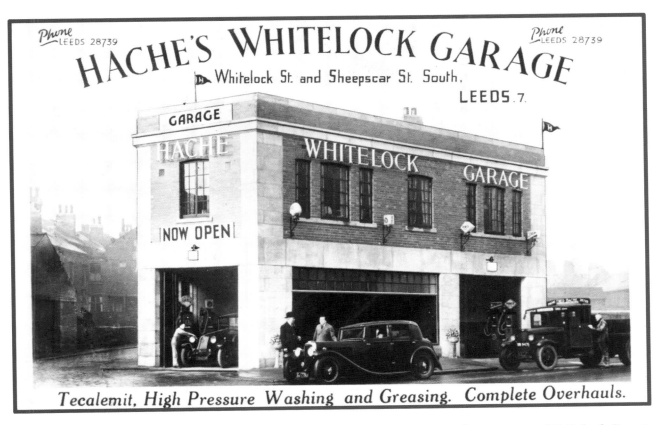

This advertising card announced the opening of Fred Hache's art deco style garage at Whitelock Street, Sheepscar, in December 1934. The car in the centre of the picture is an Alvis and on the left a Renault. Fred Hache was in business from 1934 to 1952. *Fred Hache*

Keep this as a SOUVENIR of the BATTLE for BRITAIN
Photograph by courtesy of " The Yorkshire Evening News." October 9th, 1940.

This is an advertising card published in 1940. On the back is printed: "These Souvenir photographs are issued by Coldstart Petroleum Products of Bramley, Leeds, and are 2d. each. The _entire_ proceeds of sale will be devoted to the Yorkshire Evening News "City of Leeds Spitfire Fund." *Yorkshire Evening News*

Not a postcard, but of Chapel Allerton interest. This shop at 194 Harrogate Road, Chapel Allerton, was purchased by the writer's father from Thrift Stores Ltd., grocers, on 24 August 1959. The shop opened on 24 October of that year and specialised in high performance equipment for sports cars. In 1961 it was renamed the Rally and Speed Shop and was run by the writer's brother, Robert. It was then let to a tenant, latterly David Lee, and closed on 4 February 2004 when the tenant retired. It was sold on the 12th of the following month and reopened as an internet café. From 1959 to 2004 it is believed to have been the only specialist shop of this type in the whole of the United Kingdom. Outside the shop is a Riley 1·5 (registration 3554 UA) owned by Tom Riall, a wholesale confectioner of Jack Lane. *Author*

This advertising card, postmarked 4 January 1909, was published by The Provincial Motor Cab Co.Ltd. of 4 Elmwood Mills, Camp Road, Leeds. The firm used 18-25 hp Siddeley cars "luxuriously upholstered" and charged "1s.0d. per mile and 3d. per subsequent ¼ mile". *Bemrose Dalziel Ltd., Watford*

A line of Leeds motor cabs about 1910. From the left are U 915, U 963, U 988, U 952 and U 975. All are 1909 Belsize 14/16 2543 cc 4-cylinder motor cabs. Belsize Motors were located at Clayton Lane, Manchester, and made this model of motor cab or motor car from 1909 to 1913.
Unknown publisher, Courtesy L.Fish

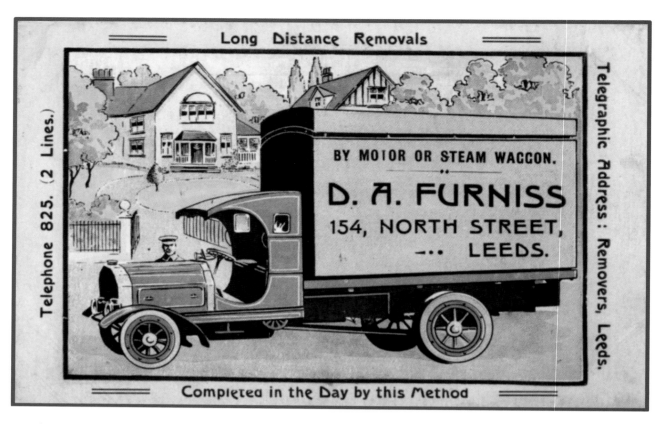

About 1912 D.A. Furniss of North Street published this advertising card of one of his removal vans.
D.A.Furniss

Shortly before the First World War, Fields, caterer's and confectioners of Headingley, owned this van of an unknown type, registration U 2991.
Unknown publisher

This beautifully painted Model T Ford van, believed to be registration No. U 3701, would date the vehicle to early 1916. The van appears rather cramped for the driver. It was owned by Campbell Bros., butchers, of 59 Great George Street, a firm that existed from about 1908 to 1920. One of the most popular vehicles of all time, the Model T was built by Henry Ford for "the masses". From 1908-1927 over 15 million Model T's, popularly known as "Tin LIzzies", were built. Only the Volkswagen "Beetle" has exceeded this number.   *Unknown publisher*

Before the war and until 1928, The Grand Pygmalion was one of the best known stores in Leeds. Managed by Monteith, Hamilton & Monteith Ltd., about 1907 the firm published a few coloured postcards of Leeds, including one of its Boar Lane Store.   This view of one of the firm's lorries was taken in the 1920's. *Unknown publisher*

The Hygienic Laundry Company of Wortley had a varied selection of vehicles. They are parked at the end of Thornhill Street and the photograph is taken looking down Thornhill Place. The most modern van, NW 4156, was new in early 1924. *Unknown publisher*

A 1920's view of a Maudsley lorry supplied by Frank H. Dutson Ltd. of Commercial Garage, Gelderd Road. The photograph is taken in Albion Street, Leeds. *Unknown publisher*

The Yorkshire Post produced a number of views of the floods which took place in Leeds on 4 September 1931. The River Aire burst its banks at Crown Point and the driver of this Yorkshire Paper Stock Co. Ltd. lorry decided to rush through. The lorry has just passed the Smith's Arms in Marsh Lane. The pub was demolished in early July 1994, but the building To Let on the right was removed many years earlier.
The Yorkshire Post

In 1931 Meanwood Beck overflowed and flooded part of Monk Bridge Road, Meanwood. Two children and an E.R.Halford Ltd. van braved the flood waters. Halford were bakers and confectioners of Bradford.
The Yorkshire Post

REMOVAL & STORAGE EXPERTS.

We invite you to inspect our Store Rooms.   Estimates without obligation.

A line up of removal vans owned by Grimshaw and Evans of Wade Lane.   The van nearest to the camera. UB 495?, is a Guy and the two adjacent vehicles UA 7093 and UA 4670 are Dennis vans.   The date: about 1930-1.
Unknown publisher, Courtesy L.Fish

A three-wheel Turog bread van, UG 143, owned by Wilson's of the Clock Buildings, Harehills.   The bread van was new in early 1932.
Unknown publisher, Courtesy L.Fish

An advertising postcard showing U 996, an early convertible lorry/charabanc owned by Bridge Garage, Briggate. The vehicle was new in 1909 and was a Halley 28/34 h.p. and described on the rear as a "Royal Blue Motor Charabanc comfortably upholstered, 15 miles per hour. Fare for 18 passengers 1 1/2 d. per person per mile or by special arrangement". In June 1913 Bridge Garage and this and other vehicles were bought by Samuel Ledgard, the well known Leeds bus proprietor. *Bridge Garage, Briggate*

City Square, 1921 with Heaps Tours charabancs. The Dennis charabanc in the foreground is U 1341, first registered 1910 and acquired second hand by Heaps Tours in March 1921. *Unknown publisher*

This advertising postcard shows Karrier charabanc U 1929 at Brunswick Garage, (off North Street), Leeds.   The card is postmarked 18 September 1912.   *Brunswick Garage*

A 1921 staff outing by Jackson Boilers Ltd. of Fullerton Park, Elland Road, Leeds.   The Albion charabanc, U 6398, is in Infirmary Street.   *Unknown publisher*

Palladium U 6479 as used by Morley Technical School in 1921. The Palladium was an American vehicle and there were several about after the First World War. Some Palladium lorries were converted into charabancs and this is an example.   The vehicle was first registered in early 1920.   *Unknown publisher*

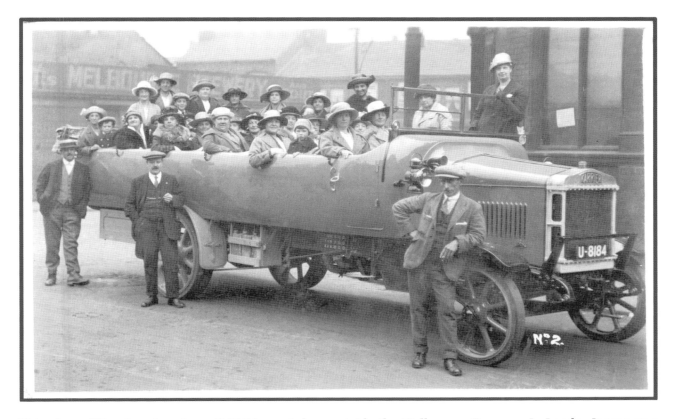

This view of Karrier charabanc U 8184 was taken outside the Melbourne Brewery In Leeds. It was on a ladies' outing in the middle 1920's. The vehicle was built in 1920. "Mam" wrote: "This is the chara we went to Scarborough in. You will know most of them no doubt."   *Unknown publisher*

Early postcards of Leeds buses and trolley buses which have not been previously published by the LTHS are almost impossible to find and hence few are included. The opening of the Moortown to Shadwell motor bus service on 30 October 1913 generated a few postcards including this postcard made from an official Leeds City Tramways photograph. It shows U 2379, a 40 hp four cylinder Tilling Stevens bus. The 24-seat body had been taken from a withdrawn Ryknield bus U 327.   *Unknown publisher*

Issued at the same time as the view above, this postcard shows the other bus used on the Moortown-Shadwell service, U 2380, a Daimler double decker.   Both U 2379 and U 2380 had short lives as motor buses. In August 1914 the Tilling Stevens was commandeered by the hospital authorities for use as an ambulance and on 5 June 1915 U 2380 was taken out of service and converted into a motor derrick. There were complaints from Shadwell. Another bus was acquired and it was not until 15 November 1915 that the bus service was restored. It ran irregularly during the War.   *Unknown publisher*

The Farnley – Willow Road bus route was opened on 1 April 1922 and in 1923 six 16-seat Guy buses (NW 1852-57) were purchased for the service. This view shows NW 1853 at the Farnley terminus. NW 1853 was first registered on 12 April 1923 and ran until February 1927.   *C. Haxby, Farnley*

A rare view of an experimental one-off streamlined Leeds bus No.200, an AEC Regent with an all metal Roe body, pictured in 1939 soon after the closure of the Pudsey tram route. It is in Church Lane, Pudsey, on service 65, Central Bus Station-Pudsey.   Bus 200 (CNW 901) was exhibited at the Commercial Motor Show in 1935 and entered service on 1 January 1936. Originally full fronted as above it was converted into a half cab in 1942. In July 1941 it was loaned to Hull Corporation on war duties. It was withdrawn on 31 January 1949.   It was sold in March 1950 and in July 1951 was seen as a mobile caravan in Brough, Westmorland.
                                                                                          Unknown publisher

INFIRMARY STREET, LEEDS

A view of AEC Regent III 664 in Infirmary Street about 1953. Bus 664 entered passenger service on 9 August 1952 and ran until 23 June 1969. *Chadwick GBL/61 Chadwick Studios, Leeds*

Vicar Lane looking north

Photograph by Ralph Smith ARPS

Very few postcards include motor buses, but this fine modern postcard shows Black Prince bus 818 in Vicar Lane. It was one of 12 Leeds cards published by Wheatfields Hospice, Headingley, Leeds, about 1999 and printed by the old established postcard firm, Judges of Hastings.   Black Prince was a company that operated from Morley and ran buses to Leeds and in the Morley area. The firm existed from 1969 to 31 July 2005 when it was taken over by First West Yorkshire Ltd.   It began bus operation upon deregulation of bus services in October 1986.   818 (P818 AWT) was acquired by Black Prince in April 1998 and was a Scania L113CRL new in April 1997 with an East Lancs B49F body and lasted until the takeover in 2005. It was allocated the First Group Bus fleet number 64818. *Wheatfields Hospice*

Several postcards and photographs were taken of the inauguration of the trackless system to Farnley Moor Top on 20 June 1911. Cars 503 and 501 are pictured in Thirsk Row at the start of the journey to Moor Top. A Bradford tram on the Bradford and Leeds through service is in Wellington Street in the background.
Leeds City Tramways

Trackless cars 501-504 were supplied by The Railless Electric Traction Company and were the first to run to Farnley. Car 503 features on many postcards and is seen at the Farnley Moor Top terminus. It was withdrawn in 1919.
Unknown publisher

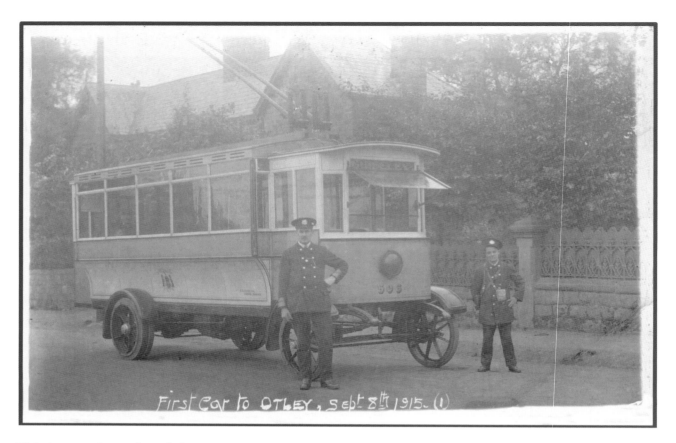

This is one of a series of three postcards issued to mark the opening of the Guiseley to Otley trackless route. Bradford-Brown cars 506 and 507 were the first vehicles. The driver was T.W. Collinson. Elsie who sent this postcard was not interested. She wrote to Ida "We are coming to Laisterdyke tomorrow and we are going to call at your house to see about our hats for the winter. I've thought of having black velvet." Car 506 entered service on 10 June 1915 and on 1 January 1921 was registered U 8407. It was withdrawn on 26 July 1928.   *Unknown publisher*

The trackless extension to Burley-in-Wharfedale was opened on 16 October 1915 and William Bramley published this postcard of car 506 at the Burley terminus. The cars built by David Brown & Sons of Huddersfield from 1915 to 1921 to a Bradford City Tramways design were numbered 505-509 with an additional car, No.501 (replacing the earlier car of this number in June 1921).   *William Bramley*

In the decade before the First World War several enterprising photographers set up their tripods at a tram terminus and photographed every tram and its crew that came along. This view shows 1902 Brush car 68 at Harehills Road terminus about 1908. Four other postcards have been found taken at the same location and on the same day as the above. They show cars 166 (two views with different crews), 168 and 196. Probably no more than half a dozen copies of each postcard were produced. Car 68 entered service as an open top car on 16 May 1902 and was withdrawn on 23 August 1926. *Unknown publisher*

This view of 1904 Brush car 63 is at the York Road terminus at Halton Dial and the date is about 1910. Car 63 entered service 1 September 1904, and was withdrawn on 25 November 1926. *Unknown publisher*

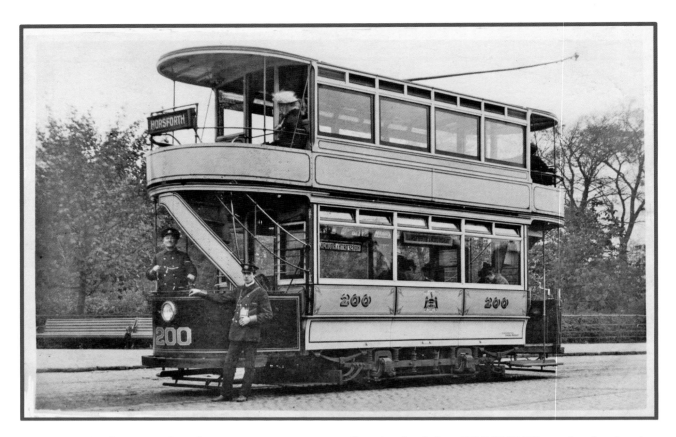

An immaculately painted Dick, Kerr car 200 at Roundhay Park. It has HORSFORTH on the destination indicator. On the back of this postcard is written, "Dad and his conductor, 1912." "Dad" has a merit stripe which indicates he had a long safe driving record, but alas his name has been lost in the mists of time.

The crew pose with Dick, Kerr car 233 at Whitehall Road terminus about 1905. Oswald Terrace is on the right. Car 233 entered service on 27 April 1901 and withdrawn on 9 February 1935. *Unknown publisher*

The tramway extension from West Park to Lawnswood was opened on 18 April 1913 and the rural location attracted many photographers. Over a dozen postcards have been seen, but although photographed from similar angles were not all taken on the same day. This view shows Leeds-built car 119, a "regular" on the route and then about five years old. It entered service on 25 May 1909, was vestibuled in February 1911, withdrawn in late 1937 and enclosed or "converted" becoming car 275. It was renumbered 349 in August 1948 and withdrawn on 31 January 1951. *Unknown publisher*

Roundhay Park, Harehills Road and Lawnswood were popular locations for posed tramcar postcards, but only one has been seen at Whingate terminus. This was probably due to the close proximity of the buildings which gave an undesirable "converging verticals" effect. On this view of 1902 Brush car 95 the verticals have been partially corrected on the computer. The date: about 1910. Car 95 entered service on 23 June 1902 was top covered October 1904 and withdrawn on 5 July 1932. *Unknown publisher*

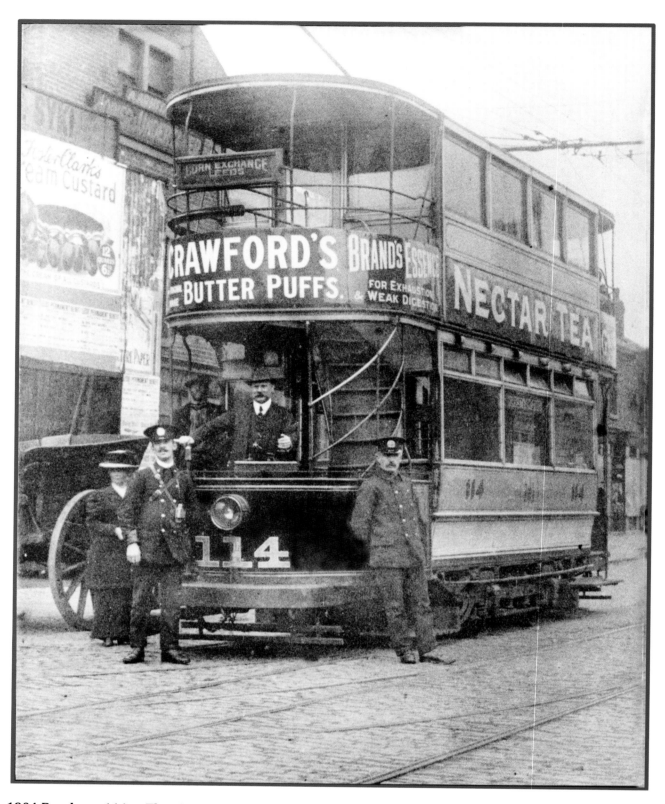

1904 Brush car 114 at Thwaite Gate, Hunslet, at the entrance to the Hunslet tram depot about 1910. The conductor is William Worsfold and at the controls is Walter Swales, the foreman at Hunslet depot. On the right is the driver Edward William Styles. At least three originals of this postcard are known to the LTHS and have survived the passage of time. Car 114 entered service on 10 November 1904, appeared with a vestibule on 4 November 1912 and was withdrawn on 28 March 1927.

The 50 cars supplied by the Brush Company through the British Thomson-Houston Company in 1902 were open top with reversed staircases. The fleet numbers had formerly been used by horse trams. The 25 cars supplied by Brush in 1904 had direct staircases and were supplied with top covers already fitted. 21 of the fleet numbers had previously been occupied by steam tram trailer cars. Of the 25 trams, Nos. 53, 54, 114 and 127 were the exceptions.

Unknown Publisher

Gaines published in large numbers three coloured postcards of the tram decorated for the Royal visit to Leeds in July 1908. Two were of a horizontal format and the other vertical. The tram is a Dick, Kerr car of 1901 with the staircases removed. This postcard was owned by John H. Gordon of Horsforth from July 1908 to 4 November 1966 when he gave it to the Leeds Transport Historical Society.   *W. & T.Gaines*

The Phototype Company and other publishers produced several real photographic cards of the 1908 decorated car. This Phototype Company version is photographed outside Kirkstall Road Works. A lot of copies of this fine, but common place card were produced. Auntie wrote to Judith that she had got " such a nice doll from the feast. This PC should be nice for your album."   *Phototype Company P6*

CORONATION ILLUMINATED CAR, LEEDS. JUNE 22nd, 1911.

For the Coronation of King George V in 1911 Gaines also published in large numbers three similar coloured cards to those of 1908. The same type of tram was used, but this one has Maley track brakes. Again, several firms published RP cards of the vehicle. *W. & T. Gaines*

THE LEEDS "PALS" BATTALION RECRUITING CAR, Sep 1914 (1). Copyright.

Dick, Kerr car 272 was decorated as a recruiting car in 1914 and a series of eight postcards of the tram were produced, but there was no indication of a publisher. No coloured postcards have been seen, but a red, white and blue colour scheme was adopted with blue muslin (possibly from the 1911 car?) predominant. A few postcards by other publishers were also produced. Car 272 entered service on 6 August 1901 as an open top car. It was top covered in February 1907 and withdrawn on 24 March 1932. This is card 1 of the series and shows car 114 in the background. *Unknown publisher*

March 31st/03. *Leeds and Bradford Express. Midland Ry.*

The Wrench Series, No. 2290

Wrench of London produced large numbers of postcards of this type, countrywide in the 1902-1904 period. This is the Midland Railway express from London St.Pancras to Leeds and Bradford and the card is postmarked 31 March 1903. The locomotive is one of S.W. Johnson's class 3P 4-4-0's of the 2606 series built in 1900 and 1901. Like all Wrench postcards it was printed in Saxony.   *Wrench Series 2290*

This is a Tuck version of the Leeds and Bradford Express and shows No.1435 a Great Northern Railway 4-4-2 Ivatt Atlantic locomotive built in 1907. It became No. 4435 in 1924. Based at Doncaster shed it was broken up at Doncaster in 1945. The 1908 postcard is a Raphael Tuck oilette (i.e. a small copy of an oil painting) in its "Famous Expresses" Series.   *Raphael Tuck & Sons. Series X No. 9972*

G. N. R. Leeds Dining Car Express. No. 275.

The Locomotive Publishing Company of London also published many post cards in the Edwardian period including this view of Great Northern Railway 275. This was an Ivatt large boilered Atlantic (4-4-2) type built at Doncaster in June 1904. It became LNER No. 3275 in February 1924 and was withdrawn in May 1945. The photograph is believed to be just north of Potters Bar. *Locomotive Publishing Co. Ltd.*

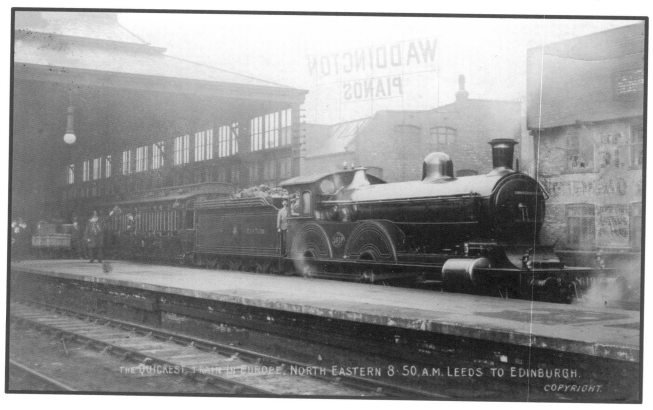

THE QUICKEST TRAIN IN EUROPE. NORTH EASTERN 8·50 A.M. LEEDS TO EDINBURGH.
COPYRIGHT.

This postcard shows North Eastern Railway M class 4-4-0 No. 1619 waiting to leave Leeds New Station for Newcastle and Edinburgh. Leeds New Station opened on 1 April 1865 when the new line across the city from Marsh Lane was opened. The locomotive was built at Gateshead in 1893, and rebuilt as a 3 cylinder compound by Wordsell's assistant, W.M. Smith in 1896. Compounding used the steam twice and was more economical. Smith's system was taken up and used by the Midland Railway for their famous compounds, one of which is preserved at the National Railway Museum at York.

Photo by J. Houghton. Published by J.Dinsdale, New Station Street, Leeds

The Phototype Company produced several postcards of local railway stations including this one of Hunslet Station in 1905. Hunslet Station was opened on 14 September 1903, replacing an earlier station a quarter of a mile away when the line was widened from two to four tracks. It closed on 13 June 1960. The locomotive is a Midland Railway 4-4-0, one of many similar classes built by S.W. Johnson. These were later rebuilt by R.M. Deeley and many survived into British Railways days in their rebuilt form.

Phototype Company 824

Pudsey Lowtown Station was opened by the Great Northern Railway on 12 April 1878 and was closed under the Beeching "axe" on 15 June 1964. The locomotive is a Great Northern 0-4-4 tank engine of a type known as a 'back' tank with the water tank at the rear of the loco over the bogie. 507 was of the GN 120 (later G2) class, built at Doncaster in April 1874 by Patrick Stirling (works No.123). It was based at Bradford shed and was withdrawn in March 1920.

Phototype Company 3601

Calverley and Rodley Station about 1910. The station opened in July 1846 as Calverley, but was renamed on 1 October 1889. It was rebuilt in 1904 when the line was quadrupled. The station closed on 22 March 1965 under the Beeching cuts. The locomotive is a 2-4-0 designed at Derby by S.W. Johnson and was working through to either Carlisle or Morecambe on the fast lines. The locomotive has been altered by R.M.Deeley (Johnson's successor) who, from 1907 onwards, fitted new chimneys and smokebox doors.
Unknown publisher

The North Eastern Railway Station at Horsforth opened in July 1850 and is still in use. The locomotive is North Eastern Railway R class No. 712. This was designed by Wilson Wordsell and built at Gateshead in 1906. It was one of the 60 strong class built between 1899 and 1907, which were the principal North Eastern Express passenger locomotives for the period.
Phototype Company 2699

Parkinson & Roy published several postcards of Cross Gates Station both RP and monochrome. This monochrome view shows a North Eastern Railway 901 class 2-4-0 locomotive. This class was built between 1873 and 1882 and lasted into the 1920's. One, No. 910, is preserved at Darlington. Cross Gates Station opened on 22 September 1834 and was closed from 1840-1850 due to the vagaries of Railway Company politics. It is still in use.   *Parkinson & Roy Studios, Leeds*

Reliable published this postcard of Cross Gates Station, looking west towards Leeds, in 1908. The locomotive is a North Eastern O class 0-4-4 tank engine, one of 110 that were built for local passenger traffic between 1894 and 1901. These later became the LNER G5 class and many lasted into British Railways days. At the time of writing a project is underway at Darlington to build several new locomotives to this design for service on preserved railways. *Reliable Series 256/12 (coloured 256/25)*

Guiseley Station opened on 1 November 1875 and is still in use. The locomotive is a Midland Railway 2-4-0 in original condition. The train is made up of one of the Midland's 5 coach sets of very comfortable clerestory bogie stock that were built specially for the Aire Valley commuter services from Leeds and Bradford to Skipton and Ilkley. Next to the locomotive is a horse box. These were always adjacent to the locomotive when in use and included a spartan compartment for the groom. *Phototype Company 1643*

The locomotive is 'Masham' an 0-4-2 Saddle Tank built by Thomas Green & Sons, Leeds (No.366). It was ordered at a cost of £825 by Harrogate Corporation and delivered in September 1904 for use on its 2ft.0in. gauge waterworks railway in Colsterdale. This line ran from Roundhill and the Leeds reservoir at Leighton to an interchange with the North Eastern Railway at Masham. 'Masham' was later taken over by Leeds Corporation for its proposed reservoir at Colsterdale which was started, but never completed. 'Masham' was sold in 1912 to Arnolds for the building of an Asylum at Colchester. The photograph was almost certainly taken in Lower Colsterdale and probably shows a party of visitors. *Unknown publisher*

'Pattie' was a 0-6-0 saddle tank engine built by Manning Wardle & Co. of Leeds in 1917, works No. 1928. It was operated by the Leeds Sand and Gravel Company at the Stourton Sand and Gravel Quarries and was bought second hand from the Ministry of Munitions at Gloucester. The quarries closed about 1930 and 'Pattie' was used during the 1920's. *Unknown publisher*

'William Black' was an 0-6-0 saddle tank locomotive purchased from Hudswell Clarke and owned by the Leeds City Tramways Department from October 1921 to August 1930. It was used in connection with the construction of the Middleton Light Railway. This postcard shows its arrival at Middleton in 1921. The sign on the right reads "Middleton Park. 18 hole putting greens. Adults 2d. children 1d." The Industrial Railway Society record that 'William Black' started life as 'The Contractor' and was one of two locomotives ordered from Black Hawthorn (No.1115) on 17 May 1895 by Walter Scott Ltd. of Leeds who had contracts in Tyneside. 'The Contractor' passed to Sir Robert MacAlpine & Sons and about 1906 to John Scott on a contract at Birkenhead. It finished up at Hudswell Clarkes' in Leeds about 1920. When it was renamed 'William Black' is not known. *Unknown publisher*

The privately run Golden Acre Park opened on 24 March 1932 and closed in 1939 for a proposed housing development which did not materialise. Around the lake was a very popular miniature railway, constructed to an odd gauge of 20 inches. The Leeds firm of Hudswell Clarke & Co. of Jack Lane built two diesel hydraulic locomotives for the line. Here we see 'May Thompson' modelled on an LNER Pacific. Today there is a short section of track and some display boards at the park to commemorate the railway. *Lilywhite Ltd. GP/L 3*

26 H.P. DIRECT DIESEL MINIATURE LOCOMOTIVE "BALTIC" TYPE
OPERATING AT GOLDEN ACRE PARK. LEEDS.

'Robin Hood' was the other locomotive used at Golden Acre Park. There was also a miniature dining car which served drinks and sandwiches. After the closure of the line the two locomotives went to Morecambe Pleasure Beach, Kilverston Wildlife and Country Park, Great Woburn and the Cleethorpes Coast Light Railway. They are both now running on the North Bay Railway at Scarborough where 'May Thompson' is renamed 'Poseidon'. Hudswell Clarke built nine of this type of locomotive. *Lilywhite Ltd.*

Canal Side, Armley.   No. 34

At first sight this placid scene seems to show a steam-powered barge on the Leeds and Liverpool Canal at Armley, but on the towpath is a horse which appears to be hauling something without any sign of draw gear or "horse marine" i.e. an attendant for the horse. The postcard was published by photographer Ernest R. Slater and he must have used some "artist's licence". The date is about 1909.   *Regal Series 34*

ON THE CANAL. RED COTE. ARMLEY.   RELIABLE SERIES   560 / 146

A more conventional view of the Canal at Armley in 1909 with Redcote Lane Bridge and a horse-drawn "flyboat". The Canal Company provided a regular service of flyboats between Leeds and Bradford, with some twenty boats engaged in the trade, until the early 1920's. This is near where a basin for coal barges was built in 1931 for Kirkstall Power Station. The basin is now a marina.   *Reliable Series 560/146*

THE "MARY GORDON" WATERLOO LAKE. ROUNDHAY PARK. LEEDS.   RELIABLE SERIES 560 / 170

Named after the wife of the then Lord Mayor, Alderman John Gordon, the 'Mary Gordon' was launched by her in 1899. 70 feet long, it was built of teak and oak by Sergeants, boat builders, Eel Pie Island, Thames. Until 1917 the electric pleasure launch was a familiar sight on Waterloo Lake in Roundhay Park. It was sold in 1923 and gave rides on the Calder from Wakefield and the Ouse from York. In 1943 it went to Brayford Pool, Lincoln. It is still there and currently being restored. It is the oldest electrically powered river boat in the U.K. This postcard was published in 1909.   *Reliable Series 560/170*

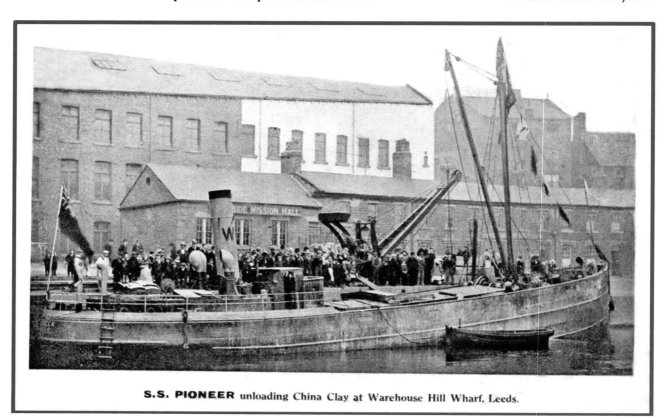

S.S. PIONEER unloading China Clay at Warehouse Hill Wharf, Leeds.

The River Aire boasted some fairly big ships at times. A large crowd is witnessing the 'S.S.Pioneer' unloading china clay at Warehouse Hill Wharf about 100 yards from Leeds Bridge. Built in 1901 by Henry Scarr of Hessle (121 grt) the ship was owned by the Wetherall Steam Ship Co., Goole, and was sold in 1911 to a Scandinavian firm. On 2 December 1932 she foundered off Norway.   *Unknown publisher*

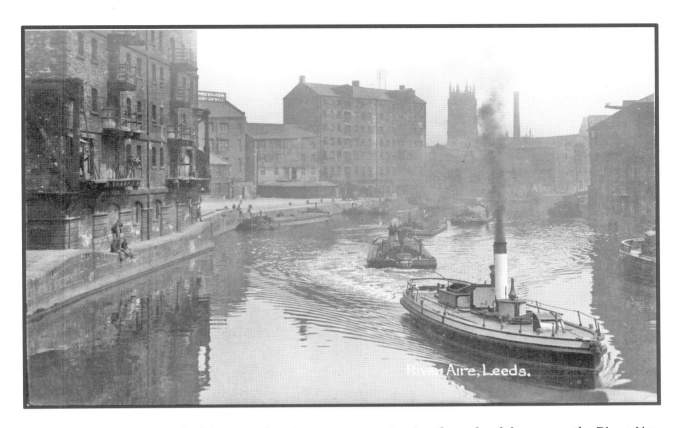

A view from Leeds bridge looking east showing a steam tug towing three dumb barges on the River Aire. There was no towpath through the centre of Leeds and a towing service was provided until the 1940's. The tug belongs to the Aire & Calder Navigation Co. and this tow is the daily one from Goole, a trip that took between 12 and 18 hours. Warehouse Hill Wharf is on the left. *Unknown publisher*

Taken from the same position as the view above, this shows the Dock Street warehouses of the Aire & Calder Navigation Company with one of the Company's boats, A.C.N. No. 4, moored outside. The warehouses were known as the "Leeds terminus" of the Company. Some of the covered dock survives as a water feature in a new housing development. Leeds Parish Church is in the background. This postcard is in the Valentines' G series and the Valentine Archive dates the card to July 1934. *Valentine & Sons Ltd., Dundee and London. G 644*

The big fire at the Great Northern Railway Hotel in Wellington Street on 26 July 1906 generated over 30 postcards by different publishers, many with greatly "exaggerated" flames. Leeds Corporation had only four steam fire engines, and was helped by the Lancashire & Yorkshire Railway Company which, "within 45 minutes" supplied by rail two engines and crews from Horwich and Newton Heath, Manchester. On the back of the postcard is written, "This is the engine from near Manchester that put the fire out". The engine appears to be a Merryweather manufactured by Merryweather & Sons of London. *W. & T. Gaines?*

Leeds Corporation obtained its first steam fire engine in June 1876, a second in 1882, third 1887 and all were built by Merryweather's rival, Shand, Mason & Co. of London. This is believed to be No.4 engine of January 1900. It is in attendance at the "Great Fire" and there is a coloured version of this postcard. A Shand, Mason fire engine stated to be ex-Leeds Corporation, (possibly No.3 of 1887), can be seen at the Armley Mills Museum, Leeds. In May 1912 No.4 engine was sold to Masham U.D.C. for £120. *W.& T. Gaines*

A steam fire engine hauled by a spirited pair of "quick hitch" horses, galloping through the cobbled streets, was one of the spectacular sights of Victorian Leeds. On the back of this postcard is written "From an album of Calverley P.C.s near Pudsey" and shows a "steamer" which has won first prize in some competition. The fire engine appears to be a Shand, Mason of the middle 1890's. *Unknown publisher*

The steam fire engines which had been used in the big fire in 1906 were described in the local press as "puny". The water pressure was "pathetically inadequate" and there was a public inquiry. In 1910 Leeds purchased its first, much more powerful motor fire engine from Dennis Bros. of Guildford. It was a Dennis "N" type and in 1913 a second similar engine was acquired. In connection with the 1914-1918 War an auxiliary fire brigade was set up which comprised five motor fire engines and crews. This 1915 line up is at the Park Street headquarters of the Leeds City Fire Brigade. *Unknown publisher*

This immaculate Vulcan was used by the "City of Leeds Gas Fire Brigade" and is "manned" by a group of school boys. It was displayed on Children's Day at Roundhay Park on 1 July 1933. The photograph was taken at Wellington Road Gas Works before the departure to Roundhay. *Unknown publisher*

The Leeds postcard publishers produced very few postcards of steam rollers, even though Leeds was a manufacturing centre for the vehicles. In 1906 "PROGRESS" was photographed. It was a road roller bought by Horsforth UDC in October 1901 and built by John Fowler & Company at Hunslet. It was a type D2 12 ton compound machine and initially allocated the registration No. 225 before becoming WR 7370 in 1921. Fowler's products carried the Leeds coat of arms as their trademark. *Phototype Company 1205*

McLaren's was another Hunslet-based company at its Midland Engine Works in Jack Lane. This engine is fitted with a belly tank under the boiler to carry extra water on long distance runs and it may well have been used to pull furniture removal vans. It is at the Wellington Inn. *Unknown publisher. Courtesy L.Fish*

This postcard shows a unique steam ploughing engine built in 1874 by John Fowler & Co. at its Steam Plough Works in Leathley Road, Hunslet. The Engine, works No.1937, built in August 1874, was the left hand one of a pair that were exported to Poland. They were fitted with special equipment to enable them to burn straw and were both driven and steered from the front. The photo is taken in the works yard and the building in the background housed the drawing office on its upper floor. The works finally closed in 1973. *Unknown publisher*

On 5 December 1931 Leeds Corporation Cleansing Department took delivery of a steam wagon from Fowlers. Works No.19708 it was registered UB 8600 and fitted with gulley emptying equipment. It served until 1942 when it was sold for scrap to Robinson & Birdsell of Moor Road. In 1968 the remains were bought by Tom Varley of Gisburn and restored as a flat-backed wagon. It is the only former Leeds Corporation steam road vehicle to survive to the present day. The date: about 1933. *Unknown publisher*

Several copies of this postcard of an accident in Woodhouse Lane on 19 July 1911 have survived. A runaway traction engine went into the front of Jesse Wilkinson's saddler's shop at No.118. Fortunately no one was hurt, and an unknown photographer recorded the scene. Altogether £150's worth of damage was done to the shop as well as to McGregors confectioners at No.120. The engine was a Fowler (works No.6851), a class B3 engine weighing 9 tons that was acquired by H.Arnold & Son of Doncaster in the early 1900's. The engine was repaired and worked for Arnolds until 1916.   *Unknown publisher*

The Yorkshire Patent Steam Wagon Company of Pepper Road, Hunslet, produced its first vehicle in 1901. The Company became the Yorkshire Commercial Motor Co. in 1911, but reverted to its old name in 1922. Steam wagon production ceased in 1937, but the works produced other vehicles until the 1970's. Unfortunately the vehicle on this fine advertising card cannot be identified precisely. The card is believed to date from about 1914.   *Yorkshire Commercial Motor Company*

CHARLIE PARKER EMPIRE LEEDS

In 1909 Humber Ltd. of Coventry, motor car and motor cycle manufacturers, opened an aircraft factory to build 50 Louis Bleriot type monoplanes. The first flight took place in January 1910, but the plane was soon obsolete and only a small number were built. By 1912 Humber ceased production. This postcard shows Charlie Parker, an early aviator with his Humber monoplane. The date is about 1910 and the event appears to have been organised by the Empire Theatre, Leeds. *Unknown publisher*

Chas. R H Pickard & Son.

"THE DESERT CLOUD"
Mrs Amy Mollison's World Famous Puss Moth Monoplane
(AMY JOHNSON)

A Souvenir of Mrs. Amy Mollison's visit to Lewis's Yorkshire Store.
FEBRUARY 17th, 1933.

Leeds

In November 1932 the well known Yorkshire aviator, Amy Johnson, broke the record then held by her husband Jim Mollison, for a solo flight from England to Cape Town, knocking 10 ½ hours off the previous record. She flew "The Desert Cloud", a De Havilland Puss Moth G-ACAB and visited Lewis's Store in The Headrow, Leeds, on 17 February 1933. The new Lewis's Store had opened on 19 September 1932.
C.R. Pickard, Leeds.

Yeadon aerodrome about 1938 with G-ABDG, a De Havilland Puss Moth, model DH80A, a high wing monoplane first registered in July 1930 and owned by Squadron Leader G.Ambler of Bradford. It was taken into RAF service on 23 July 1940 and registered AX889, It was scrapped on 7 July 1943. Yeadon aerodrome was opened on 17 October 1931, but although talked about in 1937 and 1938, did not became "Leeds and Bradford Airport" until after the War.   *B. Johnson, 265 Hyde Park Road/ L.Fish*

In 1940 to help the war effort, this Messerschmitt Bf 109 was shown in City Square.   *Unknown publisher*

This military ambulance was used during the First World War in connection with the 2nd Northern Military Hospital at Beckett's Park, Headingley, Leeds. *Unknown publisher*

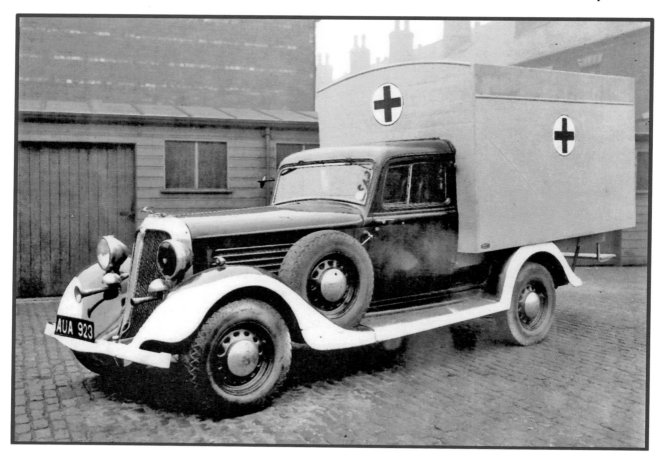

In September 1939 some saloon cars were converted into ambulances for the A.R.P. This 1934 Chrysler CA 4-door Sedan, AUA 923, is an example. *Unknown publisher*

This postcard in Boots "Real Photographic" series is almost an advertising card, About one third of the card is occupied by Boots premises in Briggate. Also on the photograph are 1902 Brush car 34 and in the background 1901 Dick, Kerr car 244. The date is 1905-6. *Boots Real Photographic Series*

A view of Briggate about 1903 showing Greenwood & Batley car 8 and a heavy dray. *Unknown publisher*

This fine, but common place card, was published by W.H. Smith & Sons in its Kingsway, (photographic) and Aldwych (monochrome) series, probably in thousands in the period from 1907 to 1910 at the height of the postcard collecting boom. Although first published in 1907, the photograph appears to have been taken in 1904 when 1902 Brush cars 47 and 74 were newly top covered.   Car 47 ran from 23 April 1902 to 5 December 1934 and 74 from 13 May 1902 to September 1930.   *Kingsway 8164*

In Edwardian times some fake tramway postcards were produced. There are postcards showing trams in Harrogate, a town which never had tramways. This rather crudely executed card shows a fictitious Aberford to Micklefield tramway and shows car 47, extracted from the view above, in Main Street, Aberford.   The background card has not been seen by the writer and is presumably from a photograph taken by the "faker".

Courtesy M. Perrins/A. Cowell

J. Valentine of Dundee, (later Valentine & Sons Ltd.) with about half a million postcards worldwide, was one of the major British postcard publishers. The firm published a modest 270 or so postcards of Leeds including this view of 1902 Brush car 84 in Briggate on its way to Roundhay. The card was one of a series of 24 Leeds postcards (Serial Nos. 67446-69 known) *registered* by Valentine in 1910. Presumably the photograph was taken in 1910 or shortly before. Car 84 entered service on 26 June 1902 as an open topper, was top covered August 1904, vestibuled February 1925 and lasted until July 1938 when it was dismantled.   *J. Valentine, Dundee , 67449*

BRIGGATE. LEEDS

This was one of the first postcards published by Harry Burniston, of Francis Street, Chapeltown, in 1922. It shows Leeds-built car 342 in Briggate bound for Headingley. Burniston published about 650 postcards including about 390 of Leeds. Car 342 entered service on 7 November 1919. It was never modernised or "converted" and last ran in February 1946. It was broken up in October 1948.   *H. Burniston No. 4*

This view in Valentine's "G" series dates from July 1934 and the photograph of Briggate shows Chamberlain car 77 bound for Horsforth. The Horsforth and Guiseley trams were withdrawn on 16 October 1934.   Car 77 entered passenger service on 17 July 1926 and last ran on 1 March 1956.
Valentine & Sons Ltd. , Dundee and London. G 646

About 1937-8 Valentine published six Art Colour cards of Leeds (A1365-70). They were copies of Valentine "G" Series postcards and this is a copy of the view above.   *Valentine & Sons Ltd. , A1369*

The major postcard publisher, Bamforth of Holmfirth, noted for its "saucy" seaside and song postcards, started postcard production in 1903 with topographical RP cards. Some were of Leeds including this view of Boar Lane with B.T-H car 181. The card is postmarked 26 June 1903. *Bamforth & Co. Holmfirth*

Dick, Kerr car 274 in Boar Lane about 1903. Trinity Church is on the right. Car 274 entered service on 5 August 1901, was top covered in March 1905 and withdrawn on 14 February 1935. *Unknown Publisher*

BOAR LANE. LEEDS.

RELIABLE ⟨WR&S⟩ SERIES 560 / 38

In 1908 William Ritchie & Sons of Edinburgh, wholesale stationers and publishers of the "Reliable" series of postcards, captured much of the Leeds postcard market with the publication of large numbers of high quality photographic type cards which did not fade. This view of Dick, Kerr car 234 was photographed passing near to Ritchies' Leeds office at 72 Boar Lane. *Reliable Series 560/38*

Boar Lane Leeds.

In an attempt to boost sales Reliable produced several versions of the view above including this decorative typically Edwardian card called a "domed oval". This postcard type first appeared in Leeds in 1909. Domed ovals were difficult to make, laminated and the coloured image was covered with a cellophane transparent sheet. A special machine and press were required to give the sculpted effect. Reliable published 12 domed ovals of Leeds in two different printings and six of Armley. Leeds publishers E.R.Slater and H.G. Glen also produced a few domed ovals at this time. *Reliable Series 560/122 and 560/207*

Over 150 different postcards of Boar Lane were published, most very common place, and a few only are included here. This is a view of Leeds-built car 121 in Boar Lane in 1909. It is unvestibuled and ran in this state for 9 months only – from 27 May 1909 to February 1910. The tram last ran in passenger service about August 1939.   This postcard was originally published by Nicholson of Leeds, but appeared later as a card published by Milton.   *Nicholsons Agency, Leeds. "N.A.L. Series"*

Excel published about 79 or 80 postcards of Leeds including this view of Leeds City Tramways-built Chamberlain car 414 in Boar Lane photographed in 1949.   Car 414 entered passenger service on 24 May 1927 and was withdrawn on 1 October 1952.   *Excel 53*

BOAR LANE. LEEDS

The only known postcard of a streamlined "Lance Corporal" tram is this Chadwick view of 273 in Boar Lane about 1952.   There were only three "Lance Corporals" (Nos.272-274) and with their luxuriously upholstered seats were very popular with passengers. Also nicknamed "Bluebirds", many passengers would not board an ordinary tram if a "Bluebird" was in sight. Car 273 entered passenger service on 13 December 1935, but in November 1954, like the other "Lance Corporals", suffered an early withdrawal because it was "Non-standard".   *Chadwick Studio Productions, Leeds, GBL/63*

BOAR LANE. LEEDS

Trams ceased to run along Boar Lane in 1956 and Chadwick were quick to remove any traces . Some postcards by Bamforth and Dennis received the same treatment.   *Chadwick Studio Productions, GBL/63*

Corn Exchange, Leeds.

RELIABLE SERIES.

From 1903 to 1907, Reliable published in large numbers about 30-40 postcards of Leeds in several different versions: monochrome, monochrome with the Leeds City coat of arms (12) and coloured and alumino types. This monochrome version of Dick, Kerr car 233 and 1902 Brush car 113 at the Corn Exchange was one which was not published with the Leeds Coat of Arms. *Reliable Series*

A Valentine view of Dick, Kerr car 267 at the Corn Exchange with a dray and 195 at the Call Lane tram stop. The date is about 1913. Car 267 entered service as an open topper on 5 August 1901, was top covered in August 1907 and withdrawn on 7 February 1927. *J. Valentine, Dundee 77934*

This is believed to be part of the memorial procession of 20 May 1910 held to mark the death of King Edward VII. The view is taken in Kirkgate with a military procession heading for the Leeds Parish Church. 1904 Brush car 88, (15 October 1904 to 7 March 1927), in the background was fitted with a vestibule in January 1913.
Unknown publisher

This Lilywhite view was published about 1927. It shows Dick, Kerr car 244 and a variety of motor vehicles. Car 244 entered passenger service as an open topper on 29 April 1901. It was top covered in February 1905 and withdrawn on 11 December 1934. *Lilywhite Ltd. LDS 127*

This view of Kirkgate shows a decorative arch across the street and a bull-nose Morris Cowley or Oxford wending its way through the crowds. The occasion is Leeds Civic Week in 1928.   *W.S.?*

The major publisher, Matthews of Bradford, produced a number of Leeds postcards.   Some of the Leeds cards are believed to be serial numbered between 7800 and 7849. They include this fine enlarged view of Leeds City Tramways-built car 361 in Vicar Lane en route to Beeston. There is also a horse and cart, motor car and a hand cart.   The date is about 1930.   Car 361 entered passenger service on 28 September 1922, it was totally enclosed or "converted" in March 1936 and last ran in service in June 1949.   *Matthews 7849*

About 1906 W. Kettlewell & Son, furnishers, published in booklet form six tear-out advertising postcards. The only one of transport interest is this view of a 1902 Brush car passing Kettlewell's premises at 29 Park Row. The other five cards are: The Boat House, Roundhay Park; City Square, Leeds; Town Hall, Leeds; Adel Church; and Kirkstall Abbey, Leeds.   *W. Kettlewell & Son*

Taking centre stage in this postcard of Commercial Street is we believe, a 1906 Enfield, manufactured by the Enfield Motor Co. Ltd. of Redditch, Worcs. It has a West Riding registration C 1934 and also on the photograph is a women pushing a handcart.   In the background is U 740 possibly a De Dion Bouton.
W. & T. Gaines Photographic Series No.29

PARK ROW. LEEDS.

This view of Park Row dates from about 1927 and shows Dick, Kerr car 280 passing the fine Bank at the corner of Bond Street. It was designed by Sir George Gilbert Scott, the well known Victorian architect, in 1863-7. The bank was demolished in 1963 and replaced by an anonymous office block. The portico to Leeds City Museum, destroyed by a bomb in March 1941, is on the left. Car 280 entered service as an open top car on 7 January 1902. It was top covered in August 1907 and withdrawn on 15 December 1931.

Lilywhite Ltd. LDS 136

10440-15

BOAR LANE, LEEDS.

ROTARY PHOTO. E.C.

There are many early postcards showing trams in City Square and we have chosen this one at the junction with Boar Lane which includes B.T-H car 147 bound for Reginald Terrace, Chapeltown Road, and 1902 Brush car 28 heading for Roundhay. Cards seen in the 10440 series are Nos. 1-27. Car 147 ran from 15 June 1900 to March 1917 when it was sold to the West Riding Tramways Company. Car 28 ran from May 1902 to 5 February 1935.

Rotary Photographic Series, London, 10440-15

CITY SQUARE LEEDS   PETER RUSSELL

In 1929-1930 Peter Russell, a photographer of Church Street, Hunslet, published postcards of Leeds, but not many have been seen. There are postcards of Moortown, Temple Newsam and some of Leeds City Centre including this view of Chamberlain car 7 in City Square on service 17 to Halton. The War Memorial, installed in 1922 and moved to a site in The Headrow in 1937, is a prominent feature on the left.   Car 7 was in passenger service for almost thirty years from 28 August 1926 to 20 July 1956.

Peter Russell

GENERAL POST OFFICE, LEEDS.   3287

About 1947 RA (Postcards) Ltd. of London published 12 postcards of Leeds (Nos.3279-3290 have been seen). Included was this post card of the General Post Office, City Square, with Horsfield car 208 on the left and Chamberlain 15 on the right.   Car 15 ran in passenger service from 13 October 1926 to 16 January 1953.

RA (Postcards) Ltd. 3287

Although this postcard was published by W. & T. Gaines in its Photographic Series it was printed for E.A. Palmer of Chapel Allerton. It shows Chapel Allerton Methodist Church on the left (demolished in 1982) and 1902 Brush car 75 returning to Headingley. The postcard was published in 1909-10, but the photograph was taken in 1903-4. This view also appeared as a Gaines monochrome postcard No. 649. Car 75 ran in service from 18 May 1902 to 7 December 1926. *W. & T. Gaines Photographic Series No. 35*

A decorative Gaines view of Harrogate Road with B.T-H. car 176 (in service from 17 November 1899 to 4 June 1931) at the junction with King Lane. The car is on its way to Moortown and the date is about 1904. Gaines also published a monochrome version of this postcard, No.898. *W. & T. Gaines*

This is one of the most interesting Leeds tram postcards and shows 1902 Brush car 51 with its experimental top cover at the Queen's Arms at Chapeltown terminus. The view is looking to the north. 51 was a "one off" and this card is part of a series of at least 40-50 postcards of Chapel Allerton published in 1905-1908, possibly by the local post office. Car 51 entered service on 17 May 1902 and was withdrawn on 23 June 1931. It lost its "odd" top cover in January 1922. *Unknown publisher*

The Queen, Harrogate Road Chapel Allerton.

An RP card with a decorative border showing Chapeltown tram terminus looking north from a different angle. Dick, Kerr car 272 is included and the date is about 1910. *Mrs. J. Todd. Harrogate Road, Moortown*

A view of 1904 Brush car 81 at Chapeltown terminus, looking south, about 1926. Arthur Steven of Chapel Allerton Post Office published probably over a thousand postcards of the Thirsk area and about 150 cards of Chapel Allerton. A few showed serial numbers in the bottom left hand corner. This is an example. Car 81 ran from 23 October 1904 to 2 February 1939. *Steven 24*

Not a Steven postcard, but Leeds-built car 356 has just passed Steven's on its way to the Chapeltown turning point. The shop and post office at 130 Harrogate Road, on the right, is well stocked with postcards and the enterprising Steven also ran a circulating library at 2d. per book, and accepted advertisements for the Yorkshire Post and Yorkshire Evening Post. He also sold children's hoops and lacrosse rackets. The date is about 1926. Car 356 entered passenger service on 15 February 1922, was totally enclosed or "converted" in July 1936 and last ran in May 1948. *Lilywhite Ltd. LDS 117*

1904 Brush car 66 at the Harehills Avenue spur, Chapeltown Road, the Reginald Terrace short working of the Chapeltown and Moortown tramway. The date is about 1908. Car 66 entered service on 11 October 1904, was fitted with a vestibule in October 1912, and was withdrawn on 23 November 1926.
Unknown publisher

Chapeltown Road in 1908 with Dick, Kerr car 237 passing the end of Sholebroke Avenue on the left and Newton Road on the right. Car 237 entered passenger service as an open top car on 12 May 1901. It was top covered in February 1907 and was withdrawn on 28 October 1929. *Reliable Series 560/252*

A 1905 view of Roundhay Road, Harehills, with car 157, an 1899 B.T-H. car, (24 November 1899 to 15 December 1931), and 86, a 1902 Brush car, (26 June 1902 to 20 May 1927). About 1910 the houses on the left were converted into a parade of shops known as Harehills Parade. See page 93. The shops are still there. *Phototype Company 37*

A posed view of Greenwood & Batley car 13 with driver and conductor at Roundhay Park about 1910. Car 13 was new in 1897 and was fitted with a top cover in October 1908. It was vestibuled in July 1913 and ran until September 1930. *Unknown publisher*

A view of Oakwood Clock about 1920 with Greenwood & Batley car No. 8 proceeding to Horsforth. Car 8 ran from 1897 to 1 May 1928. It was top covered in March 1908 and vestibuled in July 1913. In November 1925 it became the first tram to be painted in the new princess blue and white livery. The clock was originally located in the Leeds Market, but was moved to Oakwood in 1913.   The monumental building in the background was a new entrance to Roundhay Park, which incorporated a tramway waiting room and toilets etc. It was opened in 1889 and regrettably demolished in October 1937.   *Colonial Series 797 (C. & A.G. Lewis of Nottingham)*

A 1905 view of Roundhay Road near Spencer Place with 1904 Brush car 81, then about one year old.
Phototype Company 675

This postcard is not what it seems. It is an advertising card for Marriott's cut price boot store at 107 Harehills Road on the corner with Conway Place. The tram shown is one of the fifty 1899 B.T-H. cars of the 133-182 series. No. 107 was a 1902 Brush car with reversed staircases. The date is about 1906.

Marriott's, Harehills

There are not many postcards which feature the Leeds City Tramways-built Chamberlain cars (Nos. 411-445). This view shows car 423 at Harehills Parade about 1928. Car 423 ran from 27 June 1927 to 18 November 1955. See page 91 for a comparative view taken about 23 years earlier.

Matthews of Bradford 7841

An early (1905) Phototype Company view of the Balm Road, Hunslet Carr, tramway terminus with the then new 1904 Brush car No.73. The tramway opened on 2 June 1905. *Phototype Company*

Postcards of Waterloo Road, Hunslet, are rare and this is the only one seen with any transport interest. J.E. Wilks cart is prominent in the foreground and in the background is a dray and a tramcar, possibly a Dick, Kerr car. On the right hand side is the Golden Gate public house, a faience (i.e. glazed stoneware) listed building. Waterloo Road was closed in October 1976 and the pub is the only thing on this photograph which still remains. The date of the postcard is 1905. *Phototype Company 792*

Dick, Kerr car 186 at the Jaw Bones about 1906. It is turning into the Leeds and Wakefield Road from Wood Lane, Rothwell Haigh, on lines built by the Wakefield and District Light Railways Company. The building on the right is the sub station to the tram depot used by the Company, which still stands. Car 186 ran from 22 April 1901 to 11 December 1930 and was fitted with a top cover in May 1908. A pair of jaw bones still exists near to those shown on the postcard.   *C. Ineson, Rothwell*

Dick, Kerr car 210 in Wood Lane, Rothwell. Unlike Leeds Corporation which paved its new tramways in granite paving setts with 18 inches of the road on either side, the Wakefield and District Light Railways Company used the minimum acceptable specification by paving the sides of the rails only. The rest of the road was macadam. The date is about 1910. Car 210 entered service as an open top car on 14 February 1901, was top covered in October 1908 and withdrawn after 37 years on 5 May 1938. *C. Ineson, Rothwell*

Dewsbury Road about 1920 with Dick, Kerr car 199. The photograph is taken near to Trentham Street.
Car 199 ran from 6 May 1901 to 1 July 1930 and was top covered in November 1908.
A Matthews, Trentham Street, Dewsbury Road

The entrance to Cross Flatts Park, Dewsbury Road, with 1899 B.T-H car 138 standing outside. The date
of the photograph is about 1908. Car 138 was in passenger service from 11 April 1899 to March 1917
when it was sold to the West Riding Tramways Company following a fire at the Castleford Depot of the
Company. The fire occurred on 5 March 1917 and destroyed eight trams. Eight Leeds trams: 133, 138,
147, 148, 163, 170, 177 and 180, all of the 133-182 class, were sold to the Company. *Unknown publisher*

The Beeston area was more popular with the Leeds postcard publishers than Dewsbury Road and a considerable number of postcards were produced. This close up view of 1902 Brush car 112 was taken at Beeston tram terminus in 1905 by local publisher, J. William Wood of Beeston. Car 112 entered service on 12 July 1902, was fitted with a top cover in December 1904 and ran until March 1932.
J.William Wood, Beeston

This superb transport postcard is one of the best published by the Phototype Company. The children are smartly dressed and the photograph was probably taken on a summer Sunday in 1905. It is at Lady Pit Street, Beeston Hill, and the tram is Brush car 60, then about one year old. In the background is a baker's van with the wording " Made at Silver Cups Bakery Carr's Malt Bread." *Phototype Company 996*

One in eleven Beeston Hill was a popular place for photographers and several postcards were published. This view shows an 1899 B.T-H. car 158 ascending the bottom of the hill about 1910. Car 158 ran from 7 December 1899 to 13 April 1927. It was fitted with a top cover in September 1912.   *Unknown publisher*

Leeds City Tramways-built car 294 at Beeston Parade about 1914.   The tram entered passenger service on 30 July 1913 and was withdrawn about 1941.   *Unknown publisher*

Postcards of the working class area of Holbeck are not common, but the Phototype Company published one or two including this fine 1905 view of Elland Road at its junction with Top Moor Side. The tram is ex-trailer car 98 in service from 2 January 1900 to 28 January 1927. J.Naylor's, newsagents, is well stocked with postcards. *Phototype Company 177*

On 2 July 1911 the first trial car at Morley Bottoms, Dick, Kerr car 237, created a lot of local interest. The driver is John Burbridge, the Leeds City Tramways, Chief Electrical Engineer. Three postcards have been seen of this event and this is the best. *Unknown publisher*

Both Dick, Kerr car 249 and a horse and cart are in Elland Road and about to turn into Church Street, Morley. Although this postcard has a serial number of 279, there is no indication of a publisher on the card. The date is about 1914. Car 249 ran for thirty years from 20 May 1901 to 4 June 1931 and was fitted with a top cover in November 1907. *Unknown publisher*

Dick, Kerr car 247 in Morley Bottoms about 1923. The colours on this Lilywhite card are wildly inaccurate. Car 247 entered service on 18 May 1901, was fitted with a top cover in December 1904, a vestibule in May 1925 and was taken out of service on 20 April 1937 after nearly 36 years. It was the tram that was driven by Sir Josiah Stamp, Chairman of the London, Midland and Scottish Railway Company at the official opening of the new Torre Road Depot on 8 April 1937. *Lilywhite MOY 8*

Queen Street, Morley, with Dick, Kerr car 255 on its way to Meanwood. Ethel who sent this card to her sister, Mrs. S. Radford in Mansfield, said she was living in the land of nod and feeling lonely. She was looking forward to seeing the dear faces of her sisters. The card is postmarked 2 January 1916. Car 255 ran from 9 August 1901 to 11 January 1928 and was top covered in February 1905. *S. Barnes, Morley*

Bruntcliffe tram terminus on the Wakefield to Bradford Road at its junction with Bruntcliffe Lane, in 1926 with Leeds City Tramways-built car 122. Car 122 entered passenger service on 27 May 1909 and last ran about August 1939. A mile from here on the Wakefield to Bradford Road, currently the A 650, was the Drighlington terminus of the Bradford City Tramways. *Brooks Series, Bruntcliffe BTF 5*

TINGLEY TRAM TERMINUS.

Tingley tram terminus at the junction of the Wakefield and Bradford Road. The date is about 1920 and Dick, Kerr car 186 is waiting to return to Meanwood.   *Unknown publisher*

TINGLEY TRAM TERMINUS, MORLEY.

A 1923 view of Tingley tram terminus taken from the sign post which can be seen on the postcard above. The tram is Dick, Kerr car 255 which is shown as a monochrome picture. The colours on the original postcard were very distorted. The building behind the tram is the Tingley bar fish and chip shop which after more than ninety years was still in business in 2012.   *Lilywhite Ltd. MOY 1*

There are quite a few postcards of the Crown Junction at New Wortley. This 1906 Phototype Company view shows Dick, Kerr car 253 en route to Lower Wortley. There are a lot of people waiting for the tram to the city centre.   *Phototype Company PCL 175*

An early RP, circa 1903, view of Lower Wortley tram terminus with Dick, Kerr car 250 in its original primrose and white livery.   The cart in the centre of the picture was owned by William A. Penny of Farnley.   Car 250 was in service from 23 May 1901 to 31 July 1931. It was fitted with a top cover in December 1904.   *Unknown publisher*

An early view of Wellington Bridge showing a Great Northern Railway dray and Dick, Kerr car 255 on its way from Wortley to Leeds. St.Philip's Church (demolished 1931) dominates the scene. Behind the large hoarding on the right is the Wellington Bridge Permanent Way Yard, formerly a steam tram depot. This is currently the site of the Yorkshire Post building. *Unknown publisher*

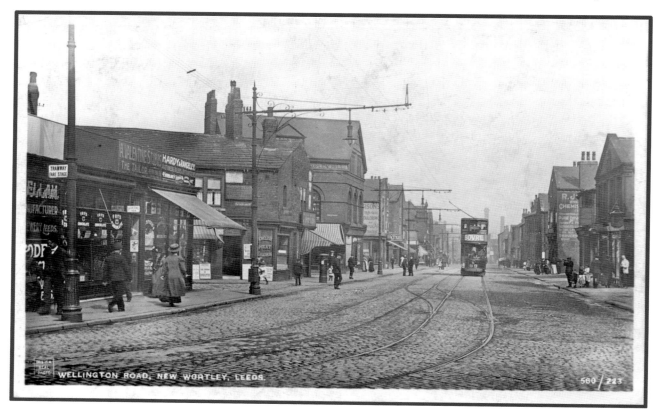

Wellington Road was generally ignored by the Leeds postcard publishers, but national publisher Reliable produced one view which shows 1904 Brush car 89 at the crossover near to the Crown Junction. The postcard dates from 1910. Car 89 was in passenger service from 15 October 1904 to 22 January 1931.
Reliable Series 560/223

1902 Brush car 94 in Tong Road at Armley Grove Place. The date is about 1904.
Unknown publisher

This fine posed view of Dick, Kerr car 253 with its crew was taken at Lower Wortley terminus about 1904. It seems that the local children had strict instructions to keep out of the photograph.   Car 253 entered passenger use on 15 July 1901, was top covered in February 1907 and taken out of service on 5 April 1927.
Unknown publisher

When the first tram (B.T-H car 155) arrived at Rodley at 5.30am on 6 July 1906, the Phototype Company's photographer was waiting. The driver was W.Booth and the conductor W.Greenfield. Second from the right is Chief Inspector Babb. Emma wrote to her Auntie and Uncle at Guiseley, "You will see from the PC we have got the cars to Rodley at last."

Phototype Company

Several postcards were produced of Rodley tram terminus soon after the tramway was opened. This one shows B.T-H. car 157 at the terminus. Car 157 was in passenger service from 24 November 1899 to 15 December 1931. It was fitted with a top cover in November 1912.

Unknown publisher

Dick, Kerr car 276 in Town Street, Rodley, about 1910. Car 276 was in passenger service for almost exactly thirty years from 13 December 1901 to 15 December 1931. It was fitted with a top cover in March 1905. *Unknown publisher*

About 1912 Metcalfe Bros. & Co. of Bramley published a number of sepia views of Bramley based on H. Graham Glen originals. This view shows Stanningley Road with a dual gauge Leeds car 109 showing LEEDS on its destination indicator. It is returning from Bradford. 1902 Brush car 109 was in service from 20 July 1902 to 29 December 1926 and was fitted with a top cover in August 1904. In 1908-9 the car had its Peckham Cantilever truck adapted for dual gauge running between Leeds and Bradford.
Metcalfe Bros. & Co. Bramley

The prolific postcard publisher, Matthews of Bradford, published about 10,000 postcards of which about 50 (believed to be serial Nos.5300-49) were of Pudsey. This photograph of Leeds-built car 308 was taken at Pudsey tram terminus about 1925. Car 308 was in passenger service from 15 January 1914 to 1941.
Matthews 5307

There are not many postcards which feature the 1931 robustly-built Horsfield cars. This is the best seen and shows car 164 at Pudsey terminus. Lilywhite Ltd. did three different printings of Pudsey postcards. This is the second printing and dates from about 1935. The first PDY 8 is "In the children's playground, Pudsey." The third PY 8 shows Fulneck Girl's School, Car 164 entered passenger service on 24 April 1931 and ran until 28 March 1959. A comparison with the view above shows that Jesse Stephenson's shop appears to have been built about 1930.
Lilywhite Ltd. PY 8

Richardshaw Lane, Stanningley, showing Dick, Kerr car 268 leaving Stanningley Bottoms. Although the tram is showing STANNINGLEY on the destination indicator, it has just left Stanningley and is on its way to Pudsey. Car 268 ran from 7 November 1901 to September 1930 and was top covered in March 1905.
Unknown publisher

Church Lane, Pudsey, in 1908 with a horse and cart and Dick, Kerr car 262. The tram was in passenger use for over thirty years from 23 May 1901 to 4 June 1931. It was fitted with a top cover in April 1907.
Phototype Company 3598

This is one of H.Graham Glen's finest tram postcards and shows Dick, Kerr car 211 at Horsforth terminus about 1907.   Car 211 ran from 13 February 1901 to September 1930 and was fitted with a top cover in December 1906.

H. Graham Glen 1541

Before the tramway was extended from Horsforth, New Road Side was a macadam road. At the distant tram terminus is 1902 Brush car 48 (12 May 1902 to 15 December 1931).

Phototype Company 2307

Over a dozen postcards were produced to mark the extension of the tramway from Horsforth to Rawdon on 26 May 1909. This view shows the then new tram, Leeds-built car 120 suitably decorated, at the Benton School Room, Rawdon. Car 120 entered use the day before the opening and ran until about August 1939.

J.K.S. ?

Photographs of trams at Yeadon are rare. This is an enlargement from a postcard showing Leeds City Tramways-built car 287 at Yeadon about 1914. It is the only known photograph of this tram. Car 287 ran from 24 February 1912 to about 1941.

Unknown publisher

At the opening of the tramway extension from Rawdon to Oxford Road, Guiseley, on 30 June 1909, Mr. Waddington, the Chairman of Guiseley Council, said it was "a day of note" and hoped it would be "a day of ever-lasting memory." The event attracted several photographers and over 20 postcards have been seen. Although the trams were of the then latest Leeds City Tramways-built 115-126 series, the crowds made sure that the individual vehicles could not be identified. This is one of the best postcards, but many of the people seem more interested in the photographer than the first tram. The card carries a serial number of 244, but there is no indication of the publisher. *Unknown publisher*

Oxford Road, Guiseley, tram terminus with 1902 Brush car 78. The date - about 1910-11. Car 78 was in passenger service from 21 June 1902 to July 1925 and was fitted with a top cover in August 1904. *Unknown publisher*

Sunlight and shadows in Cardigan Road from an original Gaines plate negative. B.T-H. car 175 bound for Balm Road is approaching. The date is about 1904 and the postcard made from this plate has not yet been found. Car 175 ran from 13 November 1899 to 15 September 1926.   *W.& T.Gaines /LTHS*

1904 Brush car 72 and a milk float at Cardigan Road tram terminus. This Richardson view was used as a specially printed removal card by Mrs. and Miss Joy and Mr. Brumfitt the new residents of "Northcliffe", the large house on the right. They moved from "Mayfield", St. Michael's Road, Headingley, to "Northcliffe" on 28 February 1910. On the back of the postcard they gave directions to the house by tram and by train from Headingley Station.   *J.W. Richardson, Post Office, Headingley*

The photographer made sure that the newly top covered tram, Dick, Kerr car 240, played a prominent part in the composition in this 1905 view of the chapel at the bottom of Cardigan Road. Unusually there is another Phototype Company postcard with the serial No. 274. It is similar to the above but shows a different tram – 1904 Brush car No. 73.   Car 240 entered passenger service on 14 May 1901 and was withdrawn on 1 November 1934. It received its top cover in April 1905.   *Phototype Company 274*

A specially posed picture in Cardigan Road taken in order to sell copies to the driver and conductor and their families. The tram is B.T-H. car 133 and the date about 1910.   No. 133 was the first of the 50 cars of the 133-182 series supplied to Leeds by the British Thomson-Houston Company in 1899.   It entered passenger service on 1 April 1899 and was one of the eight Leeds trams sold to the West Riding Tramways Company in March 1917 following the Castleford Tram Depot fire.   *Unknown publisher*

A posed postcard of 1902 Brush car 94 at Lawnswood terminus about 1920. The driver was Harry Oddy of Parkside Road, Meanwood, said to be a "real character". Car 94 ran from 23 June 1902 to 25 March 1927 and in 1903 was the first Leeds tram to be fitted with a top cover. *Unknown publisher*

One of the earliest RP postcards seen of Hyde Park is this view of open top Dick, Kerr car 234 taken in 1905. It has been enlarged from a multiview card.   Car 234 entered passenger service on 24 May 1901 and ran until 31 July 1931. It received a top cover in April 1907.   *Phototype Company 208*

Hyde Park corner with a cyclist and Dick, Kerr car 221 on its way to Chapeltown. Car 221 was fitted with a vestibule in July 1913 so this photograph was probably taken about 1910-12.   The tram entered passenger service on 26 March 1901 and was withdrawn on 1 January 1931. It received its top cover in December 1904.
Vincet Series 103/15

Chamberlain car 14 at Hyde Park about 1930. The premises occupied by the "Cosy Corner High Class Sweet Stores" on the left were formerly used by Thomas Rigby the bicycle manufacturer. See page 23. Car 14 ran from 26 January 1927 to September 1951. *Bamforth & Co. Holmfirth 101*

Horsfield car 201 appears on this postcard of Hyde Park which dates from about 1935. Car 201 was in passenger service from 30 July 1931 to 29 April 1959. *W.Robertson, Queens Road, Leeds*

Dick, Kerr car 219 in Woodhouse Lane in 1910. The tram is passing Blackman Lane. Car 219 entered passenger service on 21 February 1901 and ran until 15 September 1926. It received a top cover in March 1906.   *J. Valentine of Dundee 67454*

Of the many postcards showing trams at Headingley Oak, most very common place, we have selected this one. It is an early photographic card published by the Phototype Company and appeared about 1905. The first Phototype cards did not carry serial numbers, but it is thought that the firm produced over 300 photographic cards before 1906. This carefully posed view of Dick, Kerr car 223 at the Oak appeared in different versions and was still on sale in 1914.   The historic Shire oak tree collapsed on 26 May 1941. Car 223 ran in passenger service from 14 February 1901 to 28 October 1929 and received a covered top in March 1907.   *Phototype Company*

This postcard was published by Matthews of Bradford about 1928. The view of Leeds City Tramways - built car 343 at Headingley appeared later, c 1948, as a Lilywhite card LDS 29 (the third printing of LDS 29). The first c 1920 printing of LDS 29 was a vertical format card "The Stream, Adel, near Leeds"; the second printing of LDS 29 c 1933 shows Adel Church. Car 343 entered passenger service on 17 December 1920, was totally enclosed or "Converted" in June 1939 and was withdrawn on 10 April 1949.
Matthews of Bradford 7824

Meanwood tram terminus about 1924 with Leeds City Tramways-built car 304. Car 304 ran from 29 November 1913 to about 1941.
Hart Publishing Company No. 1455

"Before and after" postcards by the Phototype Company. This 1905 view shows a private horse-drawn carriage with coachman at Reservoir Hill, now more commonly known as Otley Road, Far Headingley. Glen Road is on the right. Compare with the postcard below. *Phototype Company 34*

The tramway extension from Headingley to West Park was opened on 11 September 1908 and the local postcard publishers were quickly on the scene. This view shows Dick, Kerr car 209 on a single track and photographed about 20-30 yards to the south east from the postcard above. It was also published as a Phototype framed card No. 4105. Car 209 ran from 21 March 1901 to 11 December 1930 and was top covered in July 1907. *Phototype Company 53A*

Gaines' photographed the same location as the previous postcard, but from the other side of the road. It shows the "tram pinch" in Otley Road before the road was widened in early 1910. Dick, Kerr car 207 is on its way to Chapeltown. The tram ran from 9 March 1901 to 19 March 1930 and was fitted with a top cover in November 1904.
W. & T. Gaines

The tram terminus at West Park showing car 209. The photograph was almost certainly taken on the same day as the view on the previous page.
Phototype Company 54A

At LEEDS.

JUST ARRIVED.

This is a pocket novelty card in which the central part of the card folds out to reveal 12 small monochrome postcards of popular locations in Leeds.   The card was in the Dainty Series.   *E.T.W.Dennis*

In a similar manner to the card on the opposite page, the central part of this pocket novelty card pulls out to reveal 12 small sepia postcards of popular locations in Leeds. The cards appear to have originated from the Hart Publishing Company. There is no indication of a publisher on the card. This card was sent from Mother to her daughter, Evelyn Cattermole of Norbury, London.　　　　*Unknown publisher*

This multiview postcard which has a postmark of 20 April 1906 was published by Glen & Co. In addition to a drawing of a motor car there are illustrations of eight Glen postcards.　　　*H. Graham Glen & Co.*

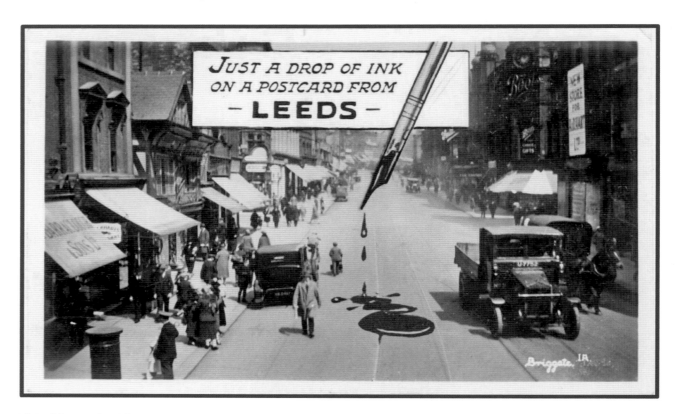

This "drop of ink" postcard was published by Bamforth & Co. and is postmarked 1 November 1928. It shows a lorry of uncertain make, U 7752, in Briggate. The registration number dates the lorry to late 1920. This card was sent from Aunt Pollie to her nephew Leslie Woolford at 22 Hill Street, Wibsey, Bradford. She hoped he liked his new school. *Bamforth & Co. Holmfirth, 1A*

A very feminine German-printed card sent with love from Annie to Mrs Day of Melbourne, York, on 17 May 1914. Annie was "delighted with the dress, but the waist would be better nearly an inch tighter." *Corona Publishing Company, Blackpool. Series 1000/1*

OUR LOCAL EXPRESS *Leeds to Pudsey*

Novelty cards similar to this were published for almost every railway in the country. The artist was "Cynicus" the 'nom de plume' of Martin Anderson, a well known Scottish cartoonist, political satirist and postcard publisher of the Edwardian period. After the collapse of his Tayport Company in 1911, Anderson moved to premises in Leeds and later Edinburgh. The card carries a postmark of 21 August 1906.   *Cynicus Publishing Co. Tayport, Fife*

This Cynicus design is less common than that above and shows a half day trip from Leeds to Headingley in 1907. It would have been a lot quicker and easier by tram! This card was sent from Maggie Burton of Hyde Park to her cousin in Warcup, Westmoreland. She said, "If you take a good look at it you will have a good laugh."   *Cynicus Publishing Company*

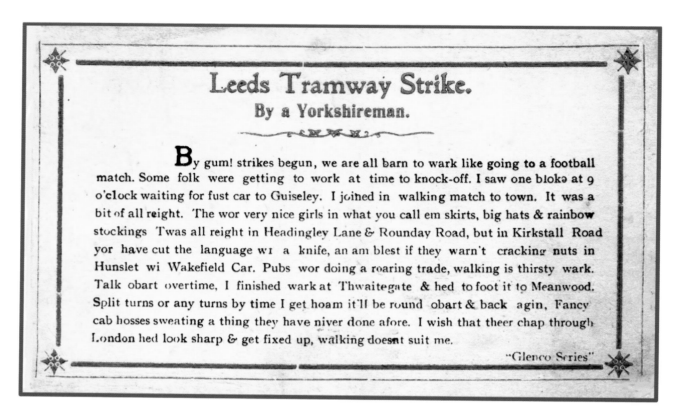

Leeds Tramway Strike.
By a Yorkshireman.

By gum! strikes begun, we are all barn to wark like going to a football match. Some folk were getting to work at time to knock-off. I saw one bloke at 9 o'clock waiting for fust car to Guiseley. I joined in walking match to town. It was a bit of all reight. The wor very nice girls in what you call em skirts, big hats & rainbow stockings Twas all reight in Headingley Lane & Rounday Road, but in Kirkstall Road yor have cut the language wi a knife, an am blest if they warn't cracking nuts in Hunslet wi Wakefield Car. Pubs wor doing a roaring trade, walking is thirsty wark. Talk obart overtime, I finished wark at Thwaitegate & hed to foot it to Meanwood. Split turns or any turns by time I get hoam it'll be round obart & back agin, Fancy cab hosses sweating a thing they have niver done afore. I wish that theer chap through London hed look sharp & get fixed up, walking doesnt suit me.

"Glenco Series"

This satirical card was published by H.Graham Glen to mark the Leeds tramway strike of December 1913. The card was sent to Private Middleton, 2 Company, 8th West Yorkshire Regiment at Marske.
H.Graham Glen & Co.

"Last car" postcards similar to this were produced for virtually every tram route in the United Kingdom. This one is for the Dewsbury Road route in Leeds and is postmarked 28 September 1907. Florrie wrote to Rowland at Hunslet. "Just an addition to your album. When you come this way do not ride the last car."
Artist F.Macleod. Published by H.G.L.

This last car postcard is less common than that on the previous page and is by an unknown artist. Annie wrote to her sister. "I hope you don't have to rush like this to get back to Morley."
National Series M.& L. Ltd 1876.

In a similar manner to Macleod, Cynicus also published "Last car" postcards for tram routes countrywide. This is the last car from Leeds and the card was posted in Chapel Allerton on 4 March 1907. It was sent with love to Miss Maggie Taylor in Harrogate from three well wishers.
Cynicus Publishing Company.

APPENDIX 1   THE LEEDS POSTCARD PUBLISHERS

NOTE. In some cases only one or two cards of a particular publisher have been seen and these are not listed. Similarly several series of cards, some of up to 50 -100 cards bear no indication of the publisher. These are also not listed.

Code of Card Types. RP Real Photographic; M Monochrome; C coloured; S Sepia - some publishers, e.g. Valentine, called sepia cards "Carbotype" postcards.

Popular locations include principal buildings, city centre streets, Adel Church, Kirkstall Abbey, Roundhay Park, Temple Newsam, etc.

LOCAL PUBLISHERS OF LEEDS POSTCARDS

Bacon, James & Sons, photographers, Leeds. M. 1903-1906.
Production. About 10 cards? of mainly special events.

Baker, Tom, Post Office, stationers, newsagents, 67 York Road, Leeds, (from 1917 at 79 York Road). In business 1903 - c 1934. Published RP postcards by February 1906 - c 1910.
Production. Over 150 cards. Some cards carry serial Nos. (highest No. seen 146) and most are now very badly faded. Cards seen are of the York Road, East End Park, city centre, Roundhay, Roundhay Park, Chapeltown, Harehills and Meanwood areas.

Bannister, Joseph, 2 and 4 Town Street, Armley. RP, RP in frame, C. c 1905 - 1926.
Production. About 40-50 cards of Armley area.

Bean, J.W. & Son. 17 Boar Lane, Leeds. S. c 1912
Production. 6 cards of city centre locations seen plus a few others.

Bishop, Eveleigh, 81-83 Briggate and 10 Swan Street, Leeds, M, S, C. 1897 - c 1903
Production. Some German-printed cards and some city centre views seen. About 20-30? cards.

Bramley, William, Electric Light Printing Company, The Woodlands, Stanks. C (few only), RP. c 1906 – c 1930.
Ceased to publish new postcards c 1930, but continued in business as a photographer until c 1936. By the late 1920's many of Bramley's cards appeared without any indication of the publisher. From about 1938 some of his cards were published by Lilywhite Ltd. and others by Mansley of Cross Gates. About 1910 Bramley acquired some of W.Hagues' negatives and they appeared as Bramley postcards.
Production. About 8,000 to 9,000 cards of more than 300 West, North and East Yorkshire villages and towns. Also two villages seen in North Lincolnshire. No cards known of central Leeds, but suburbs seen are Chapel Allerton, (about 20 cards); Cross Gates (about 90 cards); Halton and Whitkirk (about 20 cards); Rothwell (about 30 cards); Roundhay Park (about 30 cards); Seacroft (about 25 cards); Shadwell (about 20 cards); Temple Newsam (about 10 cards). Also special events cards such as Bramley Carnival etc. Most northerly cards seen Ruswarp, near Whitby; southerly, Belton and Epworth near Scunthorpe; westerly, Ingleton and most easterly, Flamborough. There are a small number of cards of Rydal and Windermere which are printed in the Bramley style.

Broomhall, H.O. 12a Market Street, Leeds. RP with matt finish. c 1919 - 1924. In business as a photographer from c 1905 to 1931.
Production. Over 200 cards. Serial Nos. seen range between 1 and 208. All are of Leeds, popular locations and suburbs.

Buckle, W. Kirkstall Post Office. M, S. c 1904 – c 1910.
Production. Probably about 12 cards of Kirkstall area.

Burniston F. Street Lane Post Office. RP. c 1924.
Production. Probably no more than about 6 cards in the area of his post office.

Burniston, Harry, (born 1890) 42 Francis Street, Chapeltown, wholesale stationer. RP type. By July 1922-1934.
Production. About 650 cards. Serial Nos., 1-602 known, but some Nos. have suffixes and some are duplicated by special events cards, e.g. the Leeds Tercentenary of 1926 (Nos. 506-527 - 22 cards). Some special events cards do not carry numbers e.g. the visit of the Prince of Wales to Leeds in 1923 (about 12 cards from 'Leeds Mercury' negatives.) About 390 cards are of Leeds. Other cards are of Yorkshire towns and villages i.e. Altofts, Airedale, Birstall, Castleford, Dewsbury, Ferrybridge, Guiseley, Harewood, Harrogate, Horsforth, Knaresborough, Knottingley, Ledsham, Ledston, Normanton, Otley, Pontefract, Scarborough, Wentbridge, Yeadon etc. The cards are mainly of popular locations with some suburban views. A few cards numbered in the Burniston series were printed for local newsagents, e.g. Wightman, Holbeck; W. Jones of Cross Flatts Park P.O. Dewsbury Road; and E.Wortley, West Park P.O.

Century Photographic Company, 43 Stratford Street, Dewsbury Road, Leeds. Real Photo Series, RP. c 1910 – 1914.
Production. Over 700 cards. The few cards seen by this firm are very badly faded and were probably printed in small numbers. They are of the Dewsbury Road, Beeston, Belle Isle, Cross Gates and Kirkstall areas. Some cards have serial Nos., (highest No. seen 709).

Chadwick Studios, 147 Roundhay Road, Leeds 8. By 1952 at 491 Oakwood Lane, Leeds 8, and later at Ingram View, Leeds 11. RP and C. 1948 - c 1970. Some cards published in conjunction with Lilywhite Ltd. which have the same serial Nos.
Production. About 100 Leeds cards, but the firm also published cards of other places in Yorkshire and the Lake District etc.

Cocker, E.W. 10 Branch Road, Armley, RP. c 1930.
Production. Probably about 6 cards of Armley.

Dawson, J.W. Bramley. RP, M. by 1904 – 1908.
Production. Probably about 20-30 cards of Bramley and Newlay areas.

Edmandson, R.W. Crescent, Halton Post Office, Leeds. RP. c 1935.
Production. Probably about 12 cards of Halton and Temple Newsam.

Fairbanks, Bramley and Pudsey. C, RP. 1907 - 1909.
Production. At least 40-50 cards of Bramley and Pudsey including 136/1-5 and 765/5-14 coloured twin views apparently published in conjunction with the Reliable Series of cards.

Fletcher, W. Lower Wortley Road. RP. c 1925 - 1932
Probably about 12 cards of Lower Wortley area.

Fountain, M. The Parade, Alwoodley Park Post Office. RP. c 1924.
Probably about 6 cards of Alwoodley.

Fowler, H. 46 Bexley Grove, Leeds. RP, S, C, Color Collotypes (6 types seen, some with highly decorative borders.) c 1905 - 1913.
In 1911 a RP Coronation Series with elaborate borders was issued.
Production. At least 100 cards of popular locations and suburbs.

Gaines, W & T. (Walter and Tom, twins born 1870), collotype and general printers. Until 1903 at Cankerwell Lane. Moved to Bankfield Works, Bankfield Terrace, Burley, Leeds, and by September 1903 started postcard production. By 1907 also had an office at 8 Upper Fountaine Street. The two Gaines lived in Burley Road and about 1910 opened an office in London. They ceased to publish new postcards after c 1913. M, C, RP.
Production. Probably about 2,000 to 3,000 cards. There are M and C versions of the same card and about 500 different views of Leeds have been seen. The remainder are villages to the north of Leeds and towns such as Bridlington, Darlington, Otley, Scarborough, Wakefield, Wetherby, Whitby, York etc. Most have no serial Nos. but there are numbered series of M and C cards, 100's York area, 400's Ackworth and Pontefract, 501-1381 (highest No. seen) many of Leeds. There is an RP series published c 1910 (Nos. seen range between 1 and 74 of which about 56 are of Leeds). There are also about a dozen RP cards with wide white borders, all seen are of Leeds. There was some sort of partnership between Gaines and J.S. Savile & Co. of Headingley. They both used the same motor car to photograph outlying villages and in some cases published the same postcards. As far as is known Gaines was the only Leeds printer to publish coloured topographical "puzzle" cards (5 seen) e.g. a view of Kirkstall Abbey with the caption "Find the Friar". Gaines published some fine Leeds tram cards of which many of the photographic plates still exist. In 1912 they published a card of the S.S. Titanic.

Geldard, Headingley. RP. c 1930.

Production. At least 6 cards of Headingley area.

Gem Art Company, Leeds. Address unknown. C, RP "H.A.L." Series and some alumino (silver effect) cards. 1905 - 1909.
Production. At least 60-70 cards. Early RP (about 30) c 1905. Later RP _H.A.L. Series (about 30). Alumino cards, 1905, (about 6?). All of mainly popular locations.

Glen, Henry Graham, Wortley. (born 1875) collotype printer, RP, M and C cards. By August 1898 to c 1928. By May 1905 at 15 Boar Lane Chambers, By September 1907 at 20 Basinghall Street, later at 133 Park Lane, by 1916 at Bagby Photographic Works, 94 St.Marks Road and finally at 106 Upper Wortley Road. Ceased to publish new postcards in bulk c 1909, but continued to produce a few new cards until c 1928. The firm remained in existence as photographers until about 1933.
Production. Probably about 4,000 cards. There are RP, M and C versions of the same view. Maybe about 500 views are of Leeds, the remainder outlying villages and cards of Yorkshire East Coast resorts, North Yorkshire, South Yorkshire, Lancashire, Belfast, Blackpool, Carlisle, Middlesbrough, Scunthorpe, etc. Cards are mainly of popular locations with some suburbs. Some cards have serial numbers and the highest No. seen is 2418. Glen also published some novelty cards.

Glen, James, Batley. (born 1873), photographer M Court cards 1897-1898 plus some later C and RP cards. Brother of H. Graham Glen and published some of the same cards.
Production. About 12 Court cards seen of popular locations plus a few C and RP cards.

W. Hague, Station Road, Cross Gates. Hague Post Card Emporium. M, C, RP. c 1905 - 1910.
Production. Probably about 200-300 cards which include Barwick, Cross Gates, Halton, KIllingbeck, Roundhay Park, Seacroft, Temple Newsam and Whitkirk. etc. Some of Hagues' negatives were taken over by W.Bramley and appeared as Bramley cards.

Hargreaves and Abe, stationers, 3 Royal Exchange Building, 43 Boar Lane, Leeds. M. 1899 - 1903.
Production. About 6 court cards plus several other cards of popular locations.

Hewlett & Green, Post Office, Kirkstall, Leeds. S. c 1925.
Production. Probably about 10 cards of Kirkstall and the Hawksworth Estate.

Hodgson, J. Cleckheaton. RP. c 1905 – 1910.
Production. Several hundreds of cards of Yorkshire villages including a few seen of Farnley, Shadwell and Scarcroft.

Holland and Vincet Series. 103 series, 578 series. Address unknown. RP. c 1912.
Production. At least 20 cards of Armley, Holbeck, Roundhay Park, etc.

Holmes & Co., 131 Chapeltown Road. RP. c 1924 - 1928.
Production. Probably about 6 cards of Chapeltown Road area.

Houghton, E.& A. & Co. Moortown. Holly Bank Series, RP. c 1910 - 1912.
Production. Probably about 12 cards of Moortown.

Hullah, J. Farnley. RP. c 1923 - 5
Production. About 12 cards of Farnley Hall and Farnley.

Johnson, Stationer, Harrogate Road, Chapeltown. M, C, RP. c 1904 - 1906.
Production. 10 Gaines cards are published with Johnson's name and he also published a further 10 or so under his own name of the Chapeltown area, plus Harewood and Arthington.

Johnson, B. 265 Hyde Park Road. RP. c 1935.
Production. 6 cards seen including one 5 view multiview. Popular locations and suburbs.

Johnson, Charles H. Call Lane, Leeds. M, C, some undivided backs. c 1901 - 1903.
Production. Probably about 6 cards of popular locations.

Kettlewell, W. & Son. 29 Park Row, Leeds. M. advertising cards. c 1906.
Production. In booklet form 6 tear-out advertising postcards of popular locations in Leeds were published.

Kirkby, E.S. 70 Brudenell Road, Leeds. M. 1906.
Production. Probably 6 cards in Hyde Park area.

Lancashire & Yorkshire Stationery Co. Ltd. 62 Boar Lane, Leeds. S, C. By 1899 (court cards) – c 1906. Retailer sold cards by Glen, Hills, Wrench etc. with L & Y name on.
Production. Probably about 30 cards of popular locations.

Liversedge, Albert, photographer, 239 Kirkstall Road. RP. c 1907 - 9. Liversedge's business appears to have been taken over by Alfred Swallow in c 1910. Both publishers used a similar logo and the backs of the cards were the same.
Production. Published a large number of mainly unidentified cards (e.g. close ups of houses, etc.) in the Leeds and Yorkshire area.

MacGawley, Richard Henry, 172 Chapeltown Road, Leeds. RP cards in frames c 1909 – 1925.
Production. Probably about 10 cards of Chapeltown area.

Machan, W.C. Kirkgate, Wakefield. RP, C. c 1910-1914.
Production. Published several hundreds of cards of the Wakefield, Barnsley and Bradford areas including 12 gold decorated cards of Leeds (Nos.213 - 224 seen, C,)

Mackie, Alex. 12 Chapeltown Road, Leeds. C, RP. c 1906.
Production. At least 6 cards from H. Graham Glen originals.

Mann, Misses. Hollybank Café, Moortown Corner, also stationers. RP. c 1924 – 1934.
Production. Probably about 12 cards of Moortown and Roundhay Park.

Mansley, Cross Gates. RP. c 1938.
Production. Probably about 30 cards of popular locations and suburbs in Leeds. Took over the production of some of William Bramley's village cards in c 1938 and published an unknown number.

Matthews, A. Trentham Street, Dewsbury Road. RP. c 1924.
Production. Probably about 6 cards of Dewsbury Road area.

Mellor, Moor Top, Armley. C. c 1909.
Production. Probably about 6 cards of Armley.

Metcalfe Bros. & Co. Bramley, S, c 1910 -1912.
Production. Probably about 12 cards of Bramley from H. Graham Glen originals.

Monteith, Hamilton and Monteith Ltd., The Grand Pygmalion, Boar Lane. C. c 1906 – 1907.
Production. About 6 cards of popular locations, including one of its Boar Lane premises.

Nicholson's Agency, 12A Queens Arcade, Leeds. N.A.L. Series. C and S gloss, color collotypes with frames and Leeds coat of arms. Some cards were printed in Germany. c 1909 - 1913.
Production. About 70 cards of popular locations plus some special events cards.

Parkinson & Roy, photographers, Kelsall Street, Leeds. M, RP. By August 1903 - 1910.
Production. Serial Nos. suggest about 600 RP Yorkshire cards plus many M cards, probably about 1,500 in total, but few seen of the Leeds central area and the usual popular locations. There are cards of Leeds suburbs: Austhorpe, Colton, Cross Gates, Halton, Killingbeck, Manston, Moortown, Shadwell, Seacroft and Whitkirk. Also many villages within a 20 miles radius to the north and east of Leeds, such as Aberford, Bardsey, Barwick, Bramham, Garforth, Sherburn, South Milford, Thorner etc. etc. Most northerly village seen Brafferton, most easterly Bolton Percy and Colton, most southerly Methley, and most westerly Leathley.

Pheasey, Joseph. 245 Roundhay Road, Leeds. RP. c 1923 -1924.
Production. Probably at least 40 cards in Roundhay Road and Harehills area.

Phototype Company Ltd., 60 Somerby Street, off Ventnor Street, Leeds. RP plus a few M and C and S in frames. By July 1904 - 1909. Ceased production abruptly in 1909, but new cards continued to appear until about 1912. These later cards, although in the Phototype

Series and style, have no indication of the publisher. Most cards up to about serial No. 3895 show the Phototype Company title on the back. A few negatives, e.g. Apperley Bridge area, were acquired by Ernest R. Slater c 1910 and appear with his name on the back.
Production. Various series of cards: 1904, a M numbered series of about 90 cards; all seen are of Leeds. 1905, an unnumbered RP series with caption apparently on adhesive tape., at least 200 cards, all seen are of Leeds. 1905-6, a RP numbered PCL series of at least 350 cards, all seen are of Leeds. 1906-12 a numbered series 1- 4554 (highest No. seen), over 1,000 cards are of Leeds. 1908-9, a series of sepia photographic cards in frames, mostly of Yorkshire villages; about 100 cards. 1908-9 A suffix series, over 500 cards, all seen are of Leeds. 1909-10 A prefix series, about 530 cards, all seen are of Leeds. These latter are in the Phototype style, but do not show any indication of the publisher. In 1909 a small number of C cards were published. The total production was over 6,000 cards of which at least 2,000 are of Leeds. The remainder are of about 150 villages and towns in West and North Yorkshire. Most northerly locations seen are of Boroughbridge and Aldborough; most southerly Horbury; most westerly Blubberhouses, Shipley and Burley-in-Wharfedale; and most easterly, York. Phototype also published special events cards, e.g. the Royal Visit to Leeds in 1908 (over 50 cards) and several carnivals.

Pickard, Charles. Photographers, 5 Park Lane, Leeds. C, RP. c 1909 - 1912, c 1934 - 1960.
Production. A series of Leeds cards 1-87 (highest No. seen) was published in 1935, but there was also an earlier "Picardo" Series of C and RP cards. and several unnumbered later cards, mainly of Temple Newsam House, Kirkstall Abbey, Leeds Girls High School, etc. Over 300 Leeds cards were published, mainly of popular locations and suburbs.

Richardson, J.W. Post Office, Headingley. M, C. By July 1903 – c 1910. Appear to be mainly from H. Graham Glen originals.
Production. About 50 cards of Headingley and Meanwood areas seen.

Richardson, George, Oakwood, Roundhay, M. 1904 – 1905.
Production. Probably about 12 cards of Roundhay and Roundhay Park.

Robertson, W. Stationer, Lending Library, 53 Queen's Road, Leeds 6. RP. c 1935.
Production. Probably about 12 cards of the Hyde Park and Woodhouse Moor area.

Rodgers, V. Leeds. C, RP. 1905 – 1910.
Production. 1905 Pictorial Postcard series C, about 20 cards of popular locations. Probably about 20 special events cards, e.g. Royal visit 1908, Proclamation Day, 1910, etc.

Russell, Peter. Grosvenor House, Church Street, Hunslet. Photographer, RP. 1929 - 1930.
Production. About 20 cards seen, mainly of Moortown, but also some city centre views.

Sandiforth, F. 129 Vesper Road, Leeds 5. RP. c 1935.
Production. About 6 views of the Hawksworth Estate.

Savile, J.S. & Co. (Joseph Sidney) 16 St. Michaels Lane and 12 Otley Road, Headingley. M, C and RP. By July 1904 - 1906.
Production. Approximately 430 cards, mainly M, of which 60-70 are of Leeds: Adel, Alwoodley, Armley, Eccup, Meanwood, Moortown, but mainly Headingley. The remainder are of about 40 villages in West, North and East Yorkshire, many in the Yorkshire Wolds. Most northerly villages seen are Wintringham and Wold Newton; most southerly Monk Fryston; most westerly Otley and most easterly Skipsea, Barmston and Ulrome. (serial Nos. seen range from 102-527).

SBW Photographic, Park Studio, Beeston Road, Leeds. RP. c 1906-1909.
Production. Serial Nos. suggest about 40 cards of Beeston and Holbeck area. (34 highest No. seen).

Slater, Ernest R. (born 1888). Basinghall Street, Leeds. RP, C, ovals, color collotypes, and others. Some printed in Germany. By August 1909 - 1910.
Production. Regal Series about 130 RP Cards (124 highest No. seen), also C oval versions, twin views etc. Cards mainly of popular locations in Leeds, but also some of Mirfield area.

Sowrey, J. Church Lane, Cross Gates. M. 1906 - 1907.
Production. At least 20 cards of Cross Gates, Manston, Seacroft, etc.

Speight E. The Stationer, 204 Harehills Lane. RP. c 1910.
Production. 4 views of Harehills Lane known. Nos. 397A, 398B, 399C and 400D.

Steven, Arthur, (born 1881, died 5 April 1956). Post Office, stationer, newsagent, lending library. RP. c 1920 (for Leeds only) - 1956. By 1920 at 52 Harrogate Road, Chapel Allerton. Moved to 130 Harrogate Road, c 1923-4.
Production. About 150 cards within half a mile radius of his post office plus some of Moortown. Earlier, Steven had been based at Thirsk and from about 1905 had published the "Steven Series" – probably about a thousand postcards of villages in North Yorkshire centred on Thirsk. "Steven Series" cards continued to be published from Steven's base at Chapel Allerton until 1956.

Stonehage, John, 5 County Arcade, Leeds. M. By 1905 - 1907.
Production. About 20 cards of popular locations.

Swallow, Alfred. Photographer, traded as E. Swallow & Co. at 24 Badminton Terrace from c 1910; at 45 Bayswater Crescent by 1912. RP. c 1910 - 1913. Appears to have taken over A. Liversedge's business c 1910. The logo and many of the backs of the cards were similar.
Production. Published a large number of mainly unidentified cards (e.g. close ups of houses, etc.) in Leeds area and Yorkshire in general.

Talbot, B. 304 Harehills Lane. Leeds. Cards appear to be printed by E.R.Slater? RP. c 1910.
Production. Probably about 6 cards of Harehills.

Taylor, W. 6 Harrogate Parade, Moortown. RP. c 1924.
Production. Probably about 6 cards of Moortown.

Thomas, W.V. 225 Dewsbury Road, Leeds. RP. c 1926.
Production. Probably about 6 cards in Dewsbury Road area.

Thompson, 54 Lower Town Street, Bramley. RP. c 1932.
Production . Probably about 6 cards of Bramley.

Thompson, E. & R. Post Office, Cookridge. RP. c 1936.
Production. Probably about 6 cards of Cookridge.

Todd, Mrs. J. Harrogate Road, Moortown. RP. (some in frames). c 1912?
Production. Probably about 12 cards of Moortown and Chapel Allerton.

Towler, 223 Stainbeck Road, Chapel Allerton. RP. c 1930 - 1932.
Production. Probably about 12 cards of Chapel Allerton area.

Waddington, John, Stourton, Leeds, printers. RP (satirical topographical). August 1965.
Production. 3 cards only known (Prospect Boulevard, Riverside Walk, and View of the Gasworks from Addington Street Toilets.)

Watson, A. Newsagent, Harehills Parade, Leeds. By 1933. RP.
Probably about 12 cards of Harehills and Roundhay Park areas.

Wheatfields Hospice, Headingley, Leeds. Printed by Judges of Hastings. C large size. c 1999.
Production 12 cards seen of popular locations.

Whitfield, H. Halton, Leeds. M, C, RP. 1904 - 1906.
Production. Probably about 40-50 cards of Aberford, East End Park, Halton, Seacroft, Whitkirk, etc.

Wilkinson, C.F. 3 Town Street, Stanningley. M, C. c 1906.
Production. Probably about 12 cards of Stanningley.

Wilson, F. Gledhow Avenue Post Office. RP. c 1927.
Production. Probably about 6 cards of Gledhow.

Wood, J. William, Beeston. RP. 1904 - 1905.
Production. Probably about 12 cards of Beeston, Holbeck and Cross Flatts Park.

Aerofilms Ltd. Bishopgate Series. RP. c 1928.
Production. This firm produced aerial photographs countrywide including about 30-40 aerial postcards of Leeds in the mid-1920's.

Bamforth & Co. Ltd. Holmfirth.   RP. By June 1903 (for Leeds) - 1904, RP and C c 1926 – c 1970.
Production. Well known for its "saucy seaside" and "song" cards, Bamforth started postcard production in 1903 with topographical views including about 12 RP cards of Leeds.   There were about 50 RP cards with Serial Nos. in brackets, c 1926.   Over 160 RP cards (164 highest No. seen.) c 1928 - 1965. About 24 RP cards with deckled edges, by 1962. 12 modern cards Colour gloss series by 1969 (1-12) seen and 6 C multiviews. (1A-6A), c 1970. Also ET 6417-6422 seen (C c 1975). All of popular locations.

Boots Cash Chemists, Nottingham. C, M, S, RP. 1903-7.
Production. 12 C cards (Nos. 526-537 seen), 1903. 12 M cards (Nos. 892-903 seen), 1903. About 24 Pelham Series, C and S (Nos. 42-62 seen). There are also unnumbered C, M and S cards and several RP cards also without serial Nos. Total production of Leeds postcards was probably about 100, all of popular locations. E. Green stationer, 15 Woodhouse Lane, sold a coloured version of Pelham cards.

Colonial Series. C. and A.G. Lewis, Ltd., 97-99 Sherwood Street, Nottingham. RP.   By August 1919 - c 1925.
Production. Serial Nos. suggest that this firm published about 3,500 postcards countrywide, with about 50-60 cards of Leeds, including Bramley, Kirkstall and Stanningley. The remaining cards are of West and South Yorkshire, Derbyshire, Nottinghamshire, London, etc.

Colourmaster International, brand name of Photo Precision Ltd., St. Albans, later at St.Ives, Hunts.   C modern cards. By 1967 – c 1980.
Production. About 24 C views of popular locations in Leeds. (Nos. PT 20161-6, 20245-20256 known) Also one or two others.

Delittle Fenwick & Co. York. C. By 1903 - c 1914.
Production. This firm published views world wide including some of Leeds c 1904 - 1906. There were night views in dark blue or brown and other cards of popular locations. 9 dark blue, and 9 brown night views have been seen of Leeds plus some alumino and C cards.

Dennis, E.T.W. Ltd. Scarborough. S, C, RP - few only. For Leeds by 1899 - c 1914, c 1952-2000. Some cards printed by Philco c 1910.
Production. 2 pre-1901 cards known. At least 30 cards, Dainty Series c 1901 - 1903 some with undivided backs. At least 32 cards (serial Nos. 3053-3064 c 1909), 20826-20835 c 1910), 22096-22105 c 1914), seen all C . Hand coloured cards about 12 cards c 1952. Modern C cards about 150. (serial Nos. LO401-460 known c 1957 "Photoblue" and "New Colour"). There is also an LT series (no captions c 1965) and a large format LO and LOO series. c 1980 - 1990's - with some copies of the earlier LO series. All of popular locations.

Durhams Ltd. Address unknown. M with red Leeds coat of arms.
Production. 6 cards seen of popular locations.

Ettlinger, Max. & Co. London E.C. and New York. C. c 1901 - 1916.
Production. Published postcards worldwide including Leeds 1102 series. About 12 cards known of popular locations.

Excel Series.   Address unknown. RP and some printed. By August 1928 (Nos.1-17); c 1934-7 (Nos.18-51); 1949 - 1950 (Nos.51A-59).
Production. Published postcards countrywide. Believed to be 79 Leeds cards, all of popular locations including at least 17 multi-views. A few cards appeared with deckled edges c 1960. Serial Nos. known 1, 1A, 2-7, 7A, 8, 9, 9A, 10-15, 15A, 16-18, 18A-D, 19, 19A-C, 20-23, 23A, 24, 25, 25A-B, 26, 27, 27A, 28-50, 50A, 51, 51A, 52-57, 57A, 58, 58A-B and 59. A six-card photogravure letter card published c 1938.

"FAB" patchwork cards. Published by W.M.Sharpe, Bradford. Part silk cards. c 1910.
Production. Published cards showing coats of arms for towns and cities countrywide including one of Leeds and a small number of views of popular locations e.g. Seven Arches, Adel, etc.

Frith, Francis, Reigate. RP and C. c 1892 (cards published by Misch & Stocks c 1901) others by Frith c 1905, c 1946-1950.
Production. A few early C and S cards have been seen. Serial Nos. suggest about 120 Leeds and 30 Headingley cards.   The Frith Archive contains 61 Leeds cards all dating from the 1950's.

Gothard, Warner, photographer, 3-7 Wesley Street Barnsley, "photographer to the Royal Family" with studios at Barnsley, Dewsbury, Halifax and 11 Park Row, Leeds. RP.
Production, 5 postcards of the 1908 Royal visit to Leeds plus about 70 mainly montage multiviews of events and disasters countrywide. Some portraits of local M.P.s etc. also published. Gothard's main activity was as a high class photographer of family portraits and groups.

Hagelberg, Wolff. Berlin. C "Hold to Light" collotype printed cards. By September 1903 for Leeds. Cards have blue background.
Production. This firm, one of Europe's finest fine art publishers, produced "Hold to Light" cards worldwide and for towns in Britain, usually in sets of 6 cards. Series 3105 (6 cards) were of Leeds. The cards are Briggate from Duncan Street; the General Post Office; New Briggate; Boar Lane; Parish Church and City Hall (i.e.Town Hall).

Hart Publishing Co. London. RP. c 1920 - 1925.
Production.   Over 460 Yorkshire cards are known. Many of these do not have any indication of the publisher, but are serial numbered and in the distinctive Hart style. Over 50 cards are of Leeds, popular locations and suburbs. Serial Nos. seen range from 1001-1462.

Hartmann, F. London. C, S, M. 1903 - 1905.
Production. At least 40 cards of popular locations in Leeds.

Hills. Address unknown. Aquatint series. C. c 1904 – 1906.
Production. Probably about 20 cards of popular locations. Printed cards for L & Y Stationery Co. etc.

Historic and Picturesque Leeds.   RP. c 1936. Distinctive cards published for cities countrywide, but publisher unknown.
Production. 6 cards seen of Leeds.

Jay Em Jay series   Address unknown. C. c 1907 – 1908.
Production. Probably about 30 cards of Leeds, Armley and Bramley, including several multiviews.

Judges Ltd., Hastings.   S. c 1912 for Leeds. Started postcard production 1902 and still in business.
Production. At least 50 cards of popular locations in Leeds printed in a sepia "artistic and atmospheric" style.

Kingsway Series. W.H.Smith & Son, Stationers. RP (Kingsway series) and M (Aldwych series). 1907. Some c1923 (S14787-96 & S15260)
Production. About 30-40 cards seen of popular locations. Aldwych cards were M versions of the Kingsway series.

Lawrence, J.F. Masons Alpha Series. Address unknown. RP. Leeds and Armley cards c June 1955 (LE1- 30) and 1957 (LE31-2).
Production. 36 cards seen of popular locations in Leeds (LE1-32) and four multiviews (LE/C/1-4), 24 cards of Armley (AR1-24) plus two multiviews (AR/C/1-2) and some unnumbered Leeds cards. The firm also published many cards for other places in Yorkshire and countrywide. A few reprinted cards had deckled edges.

Lilywhite Ltd. Halifax. RP. By July 1920 (for Leeds) – c 1962. From c 1948 some cards from views taken by Bramley and Matthews.
Production. There were four different printings of Leeds cards which _appear_ to have been as follows: 1st printing LDS1-36, 1920; LDS 37-155, 1927; LDS156-159 c 1933. 2nd printing LDS1-33 c 1933, LDS34-56? (different printing style) c 1935. 3rd printing c 1948 many distributed by Chadwick. LDS159-199 plus about 30 earlier numbers reused. 4th printing LD.G. 1-25 c 1962, large format cards with deckled edges.   About 350 Leeds cards were published.   Lilywhite also published postcards of certain districts of Leeds. i.e. Alwoodley, about 7 cards, Armley about 15 cards. Bramley about 40 cards, Cross Gates about 40 cards; Churwell about 10 cards, Golden Acre Park about 15 cards, Halton, about 10 cards, Headingley about 60 cards, Pudsey (3 different printings., about 80 cards? Rothwell, (2 different printings) about 50 cards. Shadwell about 10 cards, and Stanningley about 15 cards.

Matthews, Bradford. RP. c 1925 - 1935.
Production. Serial Nos. suggest that this firm published over 10,000 postcards of West and North Yorkshire, Morecambe and Heysham areas, Lune Valley and the Lake District. Collectors of this publisher state that postcards were usually printed in batches of 12, 25, 50 or 100 for the individual towns or districts. It would _appear_ that Leeds was allocated 50 numbers (7800-7849), Pudsey 50 (5300-5349), and Stanningley 12 (6101-6112). There are also other Leeds, Pudsey and Rodley cards, which, until more cards are seen, at present do not fit into any particular series. The firm published some fine tram cards of not only Leeds, but also of Bradford, Dewsbury, Halifax etc. From about 1938 some of Matthews cards were published by Lilywhite Ltd.

Mezzotint Company. Brighton. M. 7 July 1908.
Production. 16 cards seen of Royal Visit to Leeds on 7 July 1908.
Milton Series. Woolstone Bros. London E.C. C, RP (tinted). c 1907 – c 1928.
Production. Various series of cards. No.137 "Fac Simile" series, 198 Artlette Series, 511 Phototint series, 903 Glazette series, 1980 Glazette series (with Leeds coat of arms). These series appear to be in groups of 12 cards. There are also some other coloured cards and about 6 RP tinted cards published about 1928. Probably about 100 Leeds cards in total.
Misch & Stocks Camera Graphs Series. Graphotone Co. address unknown. C, M. 1901 - 1905.
Production. Some cards are from early Francis Frith originals (c1892) and have undivided backs. Cards are in a 512 series of which there were probably about 25 cards.
National Series, Millar & Lang Ltd., art publishers, Glasgow and London. C, M, S. c 1906 - 1907.
Production. Probably about 30-40 cards of popular locations in Leeds.
Philco Publishing Co. Ltd., (PPC Series). Holborn Place, London. Cards printed in Germany until 1914, then "British Manufacture". C, S, RP. c 1906 - 1918. Some cards also appeared as Dennis cards.
Production. Various series of cards seen 1048 C , (some cards with glitter); 2245, 2530, 2601, 2952, 4195, 4564, 4579, 4630. Some appear to be in a series of 12 cards. Probably over 100 Leeds cards in total, all of popular locations.
Photochrom Co. Ltd., Royal Tunbridge Wells. S and a few RP. c 1930 with some cards c 1950 (V series)
Production. At least 60 Leeds cards all of popular locations. Also RP cards for W.Lax, Bramley, c 1954, Nos.5540-46 plus multiview seen. Stated to have published about 40,000 postcards countrywide from 1903.
Pictorial Stationery Co. Ltd. Peacock Cards, London. Cards printed in Saxony. C. c 1901 – 1906.
Leeds serial Nos. seen range between 5466 and 5484. plus a few early cards with undivided backs and others with no serial Nos.
Production. Probably about 30 Leeds cards all of popular locations.
RA (Postcards) Ltd. (Rademacher & Aldous) 56 Ludgate Hill, London EC4. RP. c 1947 - 1948.
Production. 12 cards seen of Leeds city centre locations (Nos. 3279-3290).
Rapid Publishing Co. London, EC. RP with a few C. c 1905-1906. Some from Francis Frith originals (V135-8).
Production. Various series of cards seen; V135-138, V372 (12 cards) PS147 (18 cards with wide white borders) and PSDC 1055 series (6 cards - twin circular views with "Greetings from Leeds" and coat of arms in red). At least 41 Leeds cards all of popular locations.
Richards, R.D. and E.O. Bootham and later at Strensall, near York. RP with semi-matt finish. By April 1938 (for Leeds) - 1939. Cards on sale until the early 1960's.
Production. This firm published series of cards for many Yorkshire towns and villages, including over 400 of Leeds. (serial Nos. seen range between 1 and 399 with many cards with suffixes and some separate snow scenes of Leeds. There are separate series for Alwoodley, Bramley, Horsforth and Shadwell etc. Mainly suburban views.
Ritchie, William & Sons Ltd. (Reliable Series), 24 Elder Street, Edinburgh. Wholesale stationers from 1892 - 1958 with an office at 72 Boar Lane, Leeds, from c 1903 - 1949. RP, S, C, M, ovals, twin views, multiviews and other formats. By July 1903 for Leeds – c 1926.
Production. In many cases the same postcards appeared in several different versions. Beginning with M (30 seen) and C (also about 30) cards, there were 12 M with Leeds coat of arms, and about 12 alumino (silver effect) cards. From 1908 – c 1924 the Leeds 560 series was published (serial Nos. seen range from 1-483, but in the series there were many versions of the same card with 15 numbers seen duplicated (560/36, 87, 114-125 and 181). W. R. & S. also published a Cross Gates and Temple Newsam 256 series (256/1-42). There is also a Bramley series 136/1-5, all C twin views which were the copyright of Fairbanks of Bramley and Pudsey, and a Pudsey, Bramley and Tong 765 series (765/5-62 known). 765/5-14 were C twin views, also the copyright of Fairbanks, and the remainder were Reliable RP. Of the 560 series there were at least 232 different RP cards, 256 series 21 RP (256/1-13, 33-40) and 19C (256/14-32) and two C multi-views - 256/41-2). 765 series about 48 RP. All cards are of popular locations and suburbs.
Rotary Photographic Co. Mortimer House, Mortimer Street, London W1. RP. c 1906 - 1911 (for Leeds).
Production. About 100-150 cards in several series, (10434-10446) but with the same views duplicated many times. There were also cards with different borders, e.g. Real Photo Series etc.; twin and single views (circle plate sunk series). Mainly popular locations.
Salmon, J, Sevenoaks. RP. All about June 1952. (for Leeds). C c 1965. The firm is still in business.
Production. Over 30 Leeds cards all of popular locations. (RP serial Nos. seen range between 21251 - 21278) with some multiviews and later "Camera Colour" cards. (5 seen including one multiview)
Schwerdtleger, E.A. & Co. 28 Monkswell Street, London E.C. and Berlin. Printed in Berlin. RP (no borders). c 1910 - 1914.
Production. Believed to be about 50 Leeds cards. Known: 058-069, 0590-0609, EO2709-18, 2767-71 and 3295-7, all of popular locations.
Scott, Walter, 26-30 North Parade, Bradford. RP. 1908, c 1946-65 (for Leeds) plus a few later C. (Walter Scott died in 1948).
Production. About 6 cards of the Royal visit to Leeds in 1908 were published. At least 100 Leeds cards of popular locations and northern suburbs published from c 1946. About 1970 some coloured cards were published. This firm published thousands of cards countrywide.
Scrivens, E.L. Doncaster. RP. Royal visit to Leeds 1908.
Production. About 10 cards seen of Royal visit to Leeds in 1908. Said to have published about 15,000 postcards of South Yorkshire area.
Silvine Series. address unknown. C. By May 1906 (for Leeds) – c 1908.
Production. About 40 cards of popular locations, mainly park and woodland scenes.
Star Series. G.D. & D.L. (Gottschalk, Dreyfuss & Davis Ltd. 4 & 5 Bunhill Row, London E.C. and 45 East 20th Street, New York) Printed in Bavaria by Graphia GmbH, Munich. C. c 1905 - 1906 (for Leeds).
Production. In addition to C cards, a Celoidchrom Series was produced. It was as the Star series but with embossed borders of flowers. (4 types seen). About 40 cards of popular locations in Leeds, with two separate 6 card fold-outs were published. By September 1909 a series of RP cards of the Star Series were produced which carried the title. "The Rival Photographic Series. English Manufacture." It appears that there must have been some break up of the firm.
Stewart & Woolf, Hatton Garden, London. Cards were printed in Bavaria. M and C. 1903 - 1904.
Production. 12 Leeds cards known. Series 401 City Silhouettes (6 cards). Series 1101 M 6 cards) all of popular locations.
Taylor, A & G. (Andrew and George), London, Bradford, and 3 New Briggate, Leeds. RP, C. c 1905 (for Leeds).
Production. There was an RP series the numbering of which *implies* that there were probably about 500 Leeds area cards. There was also an Orthochrome series (C cards in frames) of about 24 cards. Popular locations and suburbs.
Tuck, Raphael & Sons, London. M, C, RP. c 1901 - 1906, c 1928 - 1934, 1951.
Production. A series of pressed and "sculpted" cards were published c 1901 (6 seen); Glosso series 1086 (6 cards); Oilette series 1781 (6 cards); Town and City Series 2014 (12 cards); Charmette Series 4755 (12 cards) all 1904-6. Then a few c 1928 - 1934 and about 40 in 1951, (RP and S). Total production of Leeds cards was over 100.
J. Valentine, Dundee. M, RP, Carbotype (sepia) and a few C cards. c 1902 – c 1965.
Production. About 270 cards of Leeds. Some isolated serial Nos. but others seen in series: 2516-20X, 2628-68. 24655-61, 24736-44, 24801-7, 27923-5, 28178-84, 40522-3, 67446-69, (1910), 75413-29, 76046-60, 77158-61, 77546-53, 77928-34, 80407-29 (Dec.1914), 89327-48 (1923), G605-14 and G642-9 (July 1934), G787-92 (August 1934), G8384-90 (April 1938), H1153-56 and H1166-68 (May 1939), K2902-9 (Jan. 1952) plus 6 Art Colour cards A1365-70 (c 1938) and a few in L and M series "Collocolour" cards c 1965. Mainly popular locations with some suburbs.
Woodbury Series. Published by Eyre & Spottiswoode. Printed in Berlin. C. By April 1904 for Leeds – c 1907.
Production. 12 Leeds cards seen, (serial Nos. 736-747).
Wrench, E. London. Printed by Markerts & Sohn, Dresden. M, C. 1902 - 1904.
Production. About 65 cards of Leeds published, all popular locations. Seen 1222-1232 M; 11534-11546 C; 11796-11804 C, 14750-14754 C; 15212-15223 C. (Some were coloured versions of the monochromes). Plus some odd Nos. and Wrench Rambler Series 0013 - 6 cards.